Stretch Out Your Hand

Exploring Healing Prayer

Kaleidoscope

Statement of Purpose

Kaleidoscope is a series of adult educational resources developed for the ecumenical church by Lancaster Theological Seminary and the United Church Board for Homeland Ministries. Developed for adults who want serious study and dialogue on contemporary issues of Christian faith and life, Kaleidoscope offers elective resources designed to provide new knowledge and new understanding for persons who seek personal growth and a deeper sense of social responsibility in their lives.

Kaleidoscope utilizes the expertise of professionals in various disciplines to develop study resources in both print and video. The series also provides tools to help persons develop skills in studying, reflecting, inquiring critically, and exploring avenues of appropriate Christian responses in life.

Kaleidoscope provides sound and tested resources in theology, biblical studies, ethics, and other related subjects that link personal growth and social responsibility to life situations in which adult Christian persons develop.

Stretch Out Your Hand

Exploring Healing Prayer

Tilda Norberg
and
Robert D. Webber

A Kaleidoscope Series Resource

United Church Press
Cleveland, Ohio

KALEIDOSCOPE SERIES

Scripture quotations are from the Revised Standard Version of the Bible, copyright 1946, 1952, © 1971, 1973, by the Division of Christian Education of the National Council of the Churches of Christ in the United States of America, and are used by permission. In some instances adaptations have been made for the sake of inclusive language and clarity. Where noted as TEV, quotations are from the *Good News Bible: The Bible in Today's English Version*, copyright © 1966, 1971, 1976, by the American Bible Society, and are used by permission. Where noted as NEB, quotations are from *The New English Bible*, copyright © The Delegates of the Oxford University Press and the Syndics of the Cambridge University Press 1961, and are reprinted by permission. Permission is given in the Leader's Guide edition Study Guide to reproduce only the author's discussion questions for group use.

Additional acknowledgment of permissions is found in the Notes section of this volume.

Library of Congress Cataloging-in-Publication Data

Norberg, Tilda
  Stretch out your hand : exploring healing prayer / Tilda Norberg and Robert D. Webber
   p. cm. —(A Kaleidscope series resource)
  Includes bibliographical references.
  ISBN 0-8298-0835-3 (student's ed.). — ISBN 0-8298-0836-1
  (leader's guide ed.)
  1. Spiritual healing. 2. Prayer. I. Webber, Robert D.
  II. Title III. Series.
  BV227.N67 1990
  234'.13—dc20   90-40777
                   CIP

Printed in the United States of America

10 9 8 7 6 5 4 3 2

United Church Press, Cleveland, Ohio

To our spouses

George D. McClain
and
Sunya Webber

How to Use the Kaleidoscope Series

The Kaleidoscope book is the basic resource in the Kaleidoscope Series for all students. For each Kaleidoscope book there is a Leader's Guide edition, which has a sixteen-page Leader's Guide bound into the back of the book. The leader will need to study both the text and the Leader's Guide to prepare to lead study sessions of the Kaleidoscope Series resources. The video is a very helpful tool for the leader and the class when using this book as a study resource.

Contents

Introduction to the Kaleidoscope Series

Through direct experience, our faculty at Lancaster Theological Seminary discovered that a continual demand exists for Christian theological reflection upon issues of current interest. To meet this demand, the Seminary for many years has offered courses for lay people. To offer the substance of these courses to the wider Christian public is the purpose of the Kaleidoscope Series.

Lancaster Seminary exists to proclaim the gospel of Jesus Christ for the sake of the church and the world. In addition to preparing men and women for the ordained Christian ministry, the Seminary seeks to be a center of theological reflection for clergy and laity. Continuing education and leadership development for all Christians focus our mission. The topics and educational style in the Kaleidoscope Series extend Lancaster Seminary's commitment: theological study reflective of the interaction of the Bible, the world, the church, worship, and personal faith. We hope that this course will provide an opportunity for you to grow in self-understanding, in knowledge of other people and God's creation, and in the spirit of Christ.

We wish to thank the staff of the Division of Education and Publication of the United Church Board for Homeland Ministries for their support in this enterprise. The Rev. Dr. Ansley Coe Throckmorton, The Rev. Dr. Larry E. Kalp, and The Rev. Dr.

Percel O. Alston provided encouragement and support for the project. In particular, we are grateful for the inspiration of Percel Alston, who was a trustee of Lancaster Seminary. His life-long interest in adult education makes it most appropriate that this series be dedicated to him. Two other staff members have guided the series through the writing and production stages: The Rev. Willard Wetzel, Project Coordinator for the Kaleidoscope Series and The Rev. Nancy G. Wright, Editor for Kaleidoscope. As a publishing staff they have provided valuable experience and counsel. Finally, I wish to recognize the creative leadership of Mrs. Jean Vieth, the Seminary Coordinator for the Series, who has been active for several years in this educational program at Lancaster.

Peter M. Schmiechen, President
The Lancaster Theological Seminary

Preface

This book was born out of our two separate Christian faith journeys. In the first chapter we tell the stories of how each of us came to explore healing prayer. Reluctant at first, with many questions and hesitations, we slowly became convinced that God heals when Christians pray for each other. Our experiences also revealed to us that we could seldom predict *how* God would work in a given situation. In addition, we observed that sometimes people stood in the way of God's healing work. From all these discoveries we share our understanding of Christian healing.

Healing through prayer sometimes raises almost as many questions as are answered. Why isn't everyone healed? What is the role of faith? Is it fair to offer healing prayer to a suffering person, only to have him or her suffer deep disappointment when the healing doesn't occur?

Before either of us began to be comfortable identifying with the healing ministry, we wrestled with these and many other questions. Yet, as we began to reflect theologically on what our experience revealed, both of us came to a greatly renewed faith in the power and love of Jesus Christ. As we moved beyond simplistic formulas, we saw how important the questions are. Chapter 1 of this book thus introduces Jesus' ministry of healing and situates healing prayer in the context of church history and our personal experience with healing. Chapter 2 deals with some of the questions that arose for us and that, we believe, may be important for other

seekers embarking on this journey of understanding the value of
healing prayer.

We speak personally about our experiences, based on years of
engaging in healing ministry and of training pastors, lay people,
and seminarians. We give readers the benefit of this practical
experience in chapters 3 and 4. There we make suggestions for
persons as they pray for their own healing and for the healing of
others. We also relate several stories of people who have been
healed in various ways (their real names and a few identifying
circumstances have been changed). We include the stories for two
reasons. First, credible stories can nurture faith. And, second,
healing is usually experienced before it is understood. As a rule,
people respond to healing with their hearts before their intellects
catch up. We invite you to hear these stories from your "heart of
faith."

The explosion of interest in healing ministry in the last fifteen
years is indicative of a way in which the Holy Spirit renews the
church. The church, we believe, is being summoned by God to
become an intentional community of healing. We see the dawn of
a new spirituality—or the revival of an old one!— which unites
concerns for wholeness of the body, mind, spirit, and emotions
with concerns for the socio-political fabric in which we live. Too
long has the church been divided between "spiritual" Christians and
"political-activist" Christians. We believe that these ministries integrally belong together. In chapter 5 we discuss the church's unique
spiritual resources for the healing of political and institutional
structures. In the last chapter, we offer a vision of the church as a
healing community and suggest some ways congregations can begin
to embody Jesus' healing ministry.

We hope this book will open a door for Christians to enter a
new phase in their faith journey. We hope it will help them look
honestly at the hard questions about healing, and discover some
answers that will free them to continue the journey. We hope that,
as Christians are emboldened to claim the ministry of personal and
political healing, the church will be renewed once again.

Most of all, we hope this book will be a catalyst for readers to
experience the healing love of Jesus firsthand—during those times
when they are in need of healing and when they are called upon to
be a channel for the healing of others. Many people have told us

that their personal encounters with the healing love of Jesus kindle joyful faith. It is happening for us. May this happen for you.

We thank the many people—friends, teachers, clients, students—who encouraged and challenged us along the way. We are especially grateful to George McClain, who read the manuscript and made countless valuable suggestions. We thank Diane Large, who cheerfully typed and retyped as revisions were made. We are grateful to Salem United Church of Christ in Allentown, Pennsylvania for providing a quiet meeting room and a good work table, and to Clayton and Margaret Swartzentrauber for their gracious hospitality. Finally, we thank those who gave permission for their stories to be told, and the many others who shared experiences of healing prayer with us.

Stretch Out Your Hand

Exploring Healing Prayer

Chapter 1

Stretch Out Your Hand

One day when Jesus was visiting a synagogue, he saw a man with a withered hand.[1] There was tension in the air. The enemies of Jesus were waiting to see if Jesus, the popular teacher and healer, would heal the man on the sabbath. If he did, they could catch him red-handed breaking Jewish law. If he refused to help the man because of sabbath laws, they could still score one for themselves. It meant they would have bullied him into doing what they wanted.

We know so well the outcome of this story. Of course Jesus chose the way of love and compassion—the truthful, risky, passionate, dramatic way that was almost guaranteed to get him into trouble. It is unthinkable to us that he would act otherwise.

He called the man to him: "Come nd stand out here [Mark 3:3, NEB]." Mark doesn't tell us how the man felt about being a part in this drama. Was he afraid? Self-conscious? Hopeful? Not daring to allow himself to hope at all? We don't know. But something was asked of him, and he said yes. He got up and moved toward Jesus.

Mark does tell us how Jesus felt. He looked at the congregation "with anger and sorrow at their obstinate stupidity [3:5, NEB]."

"Is it permitted to do good or to do evil on the Sabbath, to save life or to kill [3:4, NEB]?" Imagine those words slicing through the air with authority, cutting through the murk of the witnesses' self-righteousness, arrogance, blindness, and maliciousness. Then imagine Jesus gazing with love at the man who stood before him. Hear the gentle, yet authoritative, words: "Stretch out your hand [3:5, RSV]." *Jesus invited the man to declare himself, to act in faith on behalf of his own healing.* Again the man obeyed. When he did, his hand was restored.

1

What a story! A withered hand healed in front of people's eyes. Did this convince the opponents of Jesus of what the realm of God meant in practical terms? Not on your life. As soon as they left the synagogue, they continued plotting how to do Jesus in. Even a miracle made no impression on them. But surely the healed man, looking with amazement at his newly restored hand, was stunned.

The words of Jesus still echo through the centuries. "Stretch out your hand." Imagine Jesus saying that to you. Perhaps you can hear in these words an invitation to step out in faith—to let your intellect explore new pathways and allow yourself some experiences that might shape your faith in a new way. Maybe you, too, are being asked to act in faith for your own healing.

Or perhaps you can hear Jesus inviting you to lovingly stretch out your hand to others who need healing. If you have never put your hands on another who is hurting, never prayed for healing, this may indeed be a "stretch" for you.

Images of Healing Ministry

When we open the door to the exploration of healing prayer, we find a bewildering variety of theologies and styles in the practice of the healing ministry today. For example, most of us are familiar with TV healers, who seem to work astonishing miracles right in front of the camera. We may be intrigued by them, but we may also suspect that it is the emotionalism that "cures." We wonder what happens to the people when the high wears off. Even if we know someone who was actually healed at such a service, we may be turned off by the emotional, simplistic style of the healer. Such a healer may loudly command cancer to go away or suggest to crippled patients that they throw down their crutches. We may see people falling backward and being caught by an assistant stationed behind them. At the other end of the spectrum is a liturgical service of healing prayer, in which the pastor prays a prescribed short prayer while touching or anointing each person who is sedately kneeling at the altar rail. In addition to these two familiar forms of healing ministry, mainline Protestant churches have recently inaugurated other healing services reflecting varied styles, customs, and theologies.

These examples are from within the Christian community. But

consider the bewildering variety of New Age healers, who work with crystals, or colored lights, or even the "channeling" of spirits of the dead.

All of the people engaged in these healing practices would identify themselves with healing ministry. Is it any wonder that some of us are confused! No wonder many of us come into an inquiry of healing with certain fears and prejudices. This was certainly true for us, the authors, as we stepped gingerly into the stream that eventually propelled us into healing ministry. We tell our stories not to provide a roadmap for anyone else, but to introduce ourselves and to suggest that many other such stories are unfolding as the Holy Spirit prods the church to pray for healing. This, then, is what happened for us.

Tilda's Story

While I was a student at Union Theological Seminary in New York City, I was employed by the East Harlem Protestant Parish to work with a teenage street gang. I was greatly moved by the needs of "my kids" and by the willingness of the parish to help them. I was also attracted by the genuine devotion and worship of this congregation. They were not only people of prayer but also of action. They lived their faith. After graduation I felt called to serve God as a parish minister partly because this church gave me a vision of how vital a parish could be.

I hadn't reckoned, however, with the obstacles I would encounter in 1966 as a woman trying to serve a church. Every job exploration toward parish ministry was met with closed doors. Some of these doors slammed shut with words of ridicule and rejection. Others were shut with gentleness and concern, but still firmly shut.

The parish ministry seemed closed to me; how I yearned for it to open. I physically ached to pastor—to nurture and love a congregation—but it seemed impossible. Was there, I wondered, something terribly wrong with me? Or was the church so sexist that a woman pastor was unthinkable? Had I misunderstood God's call all along? Maybe going to seminary was just a costly mistake. I became depressed and angry.

About this time I began training as a psychotherapist, because it seemed a good way to help people and, quite honestly, because I was in so much pain myself. During the training period, I was ordained by the United Church of Christ to work in a church-sponsored community action agency on Staten Island. Within a year, the grant for the project ran out and was not renewed. With all other options gone, I threw myself into becoming a good psychotherapist, deciding that therapy would be my ministry.

After about seven years, when I was established as a Gestalt psychotherapist, I began to have vivid dreams about healing. I tried to push them away, but the Holy Spirit knows how to get the attention of a psychotherapist: Give her some dreams to chew on! Finally, I had to deal with them.

Even after exploring the dreams and admitting that God was asking me to look at healing prayer, I stalled for the better part of a year. Frankly, I was scared to death of the whole idea. Not only was I turned off by the simplistic style, the bad theology and even worse psychology of TV healers, but I was also afraid of doing anything that would cause the church to reject me again. Nor did I want to tarnish my reputation as a therapist.

But those inner nudges kept pushing me. It was clear that God was urging me to put my hands on someone and pray for healing. At last I did, but in such a way that I wouldn't have to risk very much.

At the time, I was a part-time Protestant chaplain at South Beach Psychiatric Center on Staten Island. I decided to find a patient there who was so psychotic that he or she wouldn't know what I was doing. That way I wouldn't have to make any false promises or explain anything theologically. If my prayers didn't work—and I was pretty sure they wouldn't—no one would be the wiser.

The man I chose as guinea pig for this little experiment had been in the hospital for about a year. In that time he had spoken only in "word salad"—a speech pattern in which recognizable words are tossed together in a meaningless way. Unless asleep, he chattered almost constantly.

I took him into an office and locked the door. I didn't want anyone to see this! As soon as I put my hands on his head, he stopped talking. I prayed a very simple prayer: "O God, please heal whatever caused this man to withdraw like this. In Jesus' name.

Amen." As soon as I took my hands away he started jabbering
again, and I breathed a sigh of relief. Good. It hadn't worked and I
was off the hook.

The next time I was back on that ward was several weeks later.
As I walked in, a therapist practically pulled me into his office.
"What did you do to that guy?" he demanded. I was too stunned to
speak, as he told me that the man I had prayed for had begun
talking normally that same afternoon. When asked what happened, the man reported that "the chaplain prayed for me." A
week later the man was discharged. [2]

Was I awed and joyful that God had answered my prayer so
dramatically? Not really. Well, only a little. The awe and joy came
later. Mostly I felt cornered. It was inescapable; now I would have
to explore this healing business further. And, in my "obstinate
stupidity," I didn't much want to.

However, the healing of the psychotic man was hard to ignore.
Very gingerly I began putting my hands on people to pray for their
healing: other patients in the psychiatric hospital, some friends,
one or two therapy clients. Interestingly enough, there were no
more really dramatic healings for quite a while. [3] Most people
seemed to be helped, but not totally healed by my prayers.
Sometimes a person was healed slowly over a period of weeks or
months, but faster than the doctors had predicted. In other
instances it seemed that not much changed at all for the person.
Enough did happen, however, to slowly convince me that God was
indeed using my prayers for healing. (Some other stories of healing
will be told later in the book.)

My reaction to these experiences of healing was the dawning of
a greatly renewed faith in the presence and love of Jesus. I saw him
at work in the lives of hurting people, and I saw the transforma-
tions that resulted. As I observed all this, I myself was also being
healed. I began to feel joy and humbleness at being allowed to be
part of God's healing work. At last I had found the ministry to
which I was called! The training in psychotherapy seemed to be an
important part of God's plan, not just a second-best vocational
choice. The pain of rejection by the church drained away.

As I was given a little faith and courage, the tentative begin-
nings blossomed into a new way to be a pastor. Contrary to my
expectations, I didn't lose my clients or get branded as a kook by

church circles. In fact the opposite happened. To my surprise, more people began to call me than before. I see now that people of faith are hungry to combine psychotherapeutic work with spiritual journeys. Most Christian people are eager to experience healing prayer and desire a sense of God's presence in their lives.

Bob's Story

My experience with healing prayer goes back only a few years. It is closely tied to my personal emotional and spiritual growth and also to my profession—I am a seminary professor of New Testament.

I grew up in a church that surrounded me with love, and my decision to enter the ministry was a natural one. I did well in college and eagerly looked forward to theological seminary. In many ways, I wasn't disappointed. The seminary years were the most intellectually stimulating of my life. I eagerly embraced rigorous biblical study and developed a personal theology that was strong on reason and a scientific approach to the world.

I have always been thankful for my academic training in theology, but looking back I know there was something in me that made it very hard to integrate my rational theology into my faith experience. What happened to me was similar to what happened to many like me. My theology became severed from its roots in prayer and from the practice of faith. My head and my heart became alienated.

In going on to graduate school, I found that the intense academic focus of years of study only heightened the split within me. While in many ways my life as a young adult was happy and fulfilling, I felt a lot of inner distress. I sought—and received—help in psychotherapy. Clearly, my main emotional and spiritual work at this time was to try to achieve integration of these valuable but separated inner parts.

A few years later, a family member experienced serious emotional difficulties requiring considerable time spent in a psychiatric hospital. All of us in the family suffered deeply. Consistent with my intellectual training, I did not see spiritual dimensions of this situation, nor did I do more than perfunctorily pray for my distressed loved one.

It was in this emotional state—outwardly functioning adequately but inwardly feeling pretty fragmented—that I gave some talks at a week-long summer pastors' retreat in 1984. At the same retreat, Tilda was leading what she calls a "Workshop for Wounded Healers." I sat in as she worked with the pastors one by one in a group setting.

The experience was revelatory. I saw people making rapid and significant break-throughs in emotional, spiritual, and physical healing. I witnessed Tilda's powerful fusion of psychotherapy and healing prayer. In this setting I began—for the first time in years—to pray from the heart. (I now believe that, for me, this was the most important revelation of all!)

Also, I was fascinated professionally by the way Tilda invited Jesus into people's experience as the agent of healing. What was the relation between the historical Jesus of my New Testament study and the directly experienced Jesus of what Tilda called "faith imagination"? What was the authority of the healing stories in the Gospels? The experience of this week moved me on many levels and stirred in me the need for healing in myself and my family.

The night I returned home from that retreat I had a dream in which I vividly experienced Jesus taking upon himself all the brokenness of my life. The painful memories of my life were still there, but their poison had drained away. I felt wonderfully free.

The dream, plus everything else I had experienced at the pastors' retreat, demanded action. What should a professor do? The next term I offered a short course entitled "Exegetes and Healers in Dialogue." Cautiously, I became the "exegete," and anyone interested in spiritual healing was invited to gather for a week of study and conversation.

I was amazed at the response. Students and pastors gathered from everywhere, it seemed. At the same time Tilda offered workshops through the seminary where I taught, and I continued experiencing her work. Then I set up regular workshops for pastors, seminarians, and lay persons on healing, sometimes with Tilda and sometimes by myself or with others. In this way I was responding professionally to a call to be an interpreter of and advocate for Christian healing in mainline churches.

My personal learning about the healing love of God has continued, too, although I am very much a novice in practice. Over the past few years I have been growing spiritually—at about the rate at which I am willing to allow the Spirit to work in me!

Also, I am learning something of the meaning of praying for others. The family member I spoke of is much better today, thanks to an excellent psychiatrist *and*, I believe, the prayers of many people. One evening, four of us celebrated a service of Holy Communion on behalf of this family member. Although not present, the family member nevertheless was helped. The terrible recurrent anxiety attacks stopped cold after the prayer service for a period of several days and were not as frequent after that. I knew our prayers made a difference. I don't understand the results rationally, but I keep discovering in myself and in others surprising ways God works in us when we open ourselves through healing prayer.

What I am most thankful for in this spiritual adventure is my own renewed awareness of the reality of our loving, healing God, alive in me and in the world. For me, this is the most important healing there could be.

Healing: The Church's Story

Personal experiences of healing are always shaped by individual personalities, life experiences, and a sense of call. Each person will have a unique story to tell of the ways God addresses her or his needs and gifts.

But all the stories together comprise something more. They are signs of a power that has been present in the church down through the ages and is being rediscovered in churches across the land in our own day.

But if spiritual healing has always had some part in the church's life, why does it need to be revived? Also, what happened to the church's healing ministry in Christendom over the centuries? And what factors have led to a revival of interest in healing in recent years? In order to put the present volume's approach to Christian healing in a broad perspective, there follows a brief outline of the story of healing in the historical Christian church.[4]

For the first two or three centuries of the church's existence,

Christian writers maintained New Testament perspectives on healing. Speaking for the times, the theologian Origen (died ca. 254) wrote: "The name of Jesus can still remove distractions from the minds of men, and expel demons, and also take away diseases."[5] In the Eastern church, such belief flourished for centuries and is still reflected in a service of healing based on an ancient liturgy.

Morton Kelsey identifies three reasons why healing was generally discounted in the Western church from the Middle Ages until now: a shift in conceptions of God and of human nature; the ascendance of rationalism in Western theology; and popular accounts of miraculous cures, which were often highly fanciful and strained credibility.[6] Let us consider each of these factors in turn.

1. The early theologians of the West began to downplay and even discourage the gift of healing, under the impact of a heightened sense of human depravity and divine punishment. Illness was seen either as punishment for sin or as a means to prepare the sufferer for the soul's salvation. The soul and body were separated and associated with good and evil, respectively. This-worldly, embodied existence was a source of suspicion or denial. Symbolizing the trend, the ancient practice of anointing for healing gradually became a service of anointing to prepare the soul for death.

Augustine (died 430) shared this suspicion of Christian healing, teaching that miraculous healings were signs of the apostolic age and not for his own day. Yet late in his life, partly influenced by some spectacular healings at the church altar while he was presiding, Augustine revised his views and instituted the recording and attesting of miracles in his diocese.[7]

2. Probably the most important factor in the decline of healing in the Western church was the rise of rationalism and its flowering in Scholasticism. The highly rationalized theological system of Thomas Aquinas (died 1274) allowed no real place for religious healing or the exercise of the spiritual gifts mentioned by Paul (1 Corinthians 12:4–11). Jesus performed miracles, Aquinas argued, in order to prove his teaching and to demonstrate his divinity. Physical healing was meant to lead to spiritual healing:

By how much a soul is of more account than a body, by so much is the forgiving of sins a greater work than healing the body; but because the one is unseen He does the lesser and more manifest thing in order to prove the greater and more unseen.[8]

The Protestant Reformation did not entirely break with this rationalism. Both Luther (died 1546) and Calvin (died 1564), perhaps reacting to some of the superstitious claims of the day and refuting the Roman Catholic sacrament of anointing, argued that miracles of healing were only for the time of the early church. Calvin wrote:

> The gift of healing disappeared with the other miraculous powers which the Lord was pleased to give for a time. . . . Therefore, even were we to grant that anointing was a sacrament of those powers which were then administered by the hands of the apostles, it pertains not to us.[9]

Luther also denied the gift of healing for his own day but lived, as Kelsey says, "to see his friend Melanchthon visibly brought from the point of death through his own prayers." Luther once wrote in a letter that "a cabinetmaker here was . . . afflicted with madness and we cured him by prayer in Christ's name."[10] Clearly with Luther, as with Augustine, practice was not entirely consistent with theory!

Since the eighteenth century Enlightenment, the theological climate has hardly been congenial to belief in spiritual healing! Theological voices have tended to be either hostile or, at best, guarded in their estimations of the ability or the will of God to heal through nonmedical means. Silence on the subject is perhaps the most common reaction in most theological circles.

3. When we turn to healing in popular religious practice, we find a different situation. In ancient and Medieval times, there was no lack of recourse to healing through such means as oils, prayers to saints and the use of their relics, sleeping in sacred shrines, and receiving the prayers of those deemed especially holy. Shrines such as Lourdes attest both to the persistence of the gift of healing in the church and, unfortunately, to its marginalization in the church's life.

In virtually every age of the church's history there have been those whose ministries were accompanied by healing, such as

Francis Xavier and Vincent de Paul on the Roman Catholic side, and George Fox, John Wesley, and Johann Christian Blumhardt on the Protestant. [11]

In nineteenth and twentieth century America many names are associated with ministries of healing, such as Mary Baker Eddy, Kathryn Kuhlman, and Oral Roberts. Part of the reason controversy surrounds them is that mainstream tradition lacks its own vital theology of healing with which to assimilate whatever true insights and gifts such figures offer.

The church's story of healing leaves an impression of lost opportunities. Theology and practice did not support and enrich each other as they should. At times both departed from the biblical heritage. Still, the gift of healing has persisted, but often unfortunately removed from the church's sacramental and corporate life.

Against this background, why then has there been a renewal of Christian healing in our day? Among the many factors that could be mentioned, three stand out. Two of them are broad cultural-intellectual movements; the other, an awakening of the Spirit.

1. We are in a period when the very models whereby we envision our world are in transition. In fields as diverse as physics and astronomy, medicine and biology, international politics, ecology and religion, we see a shift from mechanical to organic models, from compartmentalization toward holism. With regard to our understanding of human nature, the result has been an ever deepening appreciation for the intricate ways emotions, body, and mind influence each other. Christians are recognizing that their own heritage contains practical wisdom about health and wholeness of astonishing contemporary relevance.

2. Confidence in the ability of human reason to order existence has eroded somewhat in our day. As a result, in both academic theology and popular faith there is a greater openness to the transcendent and the spiritual. The rationalism that once easily dismissed accounts of unexplained healings is itself now seen as naive and culture-bound.

3. From within the framework of Christian faith, the gentle renewal of healing in our day comes as a sign that the Holy Spirit is at work in the church and in the world. This is evident dramatically in the ministries of specially gifted people such as

Agnes Sanford, Olga Worrall, and Francis MacNutt. More important, the Spirit's work is evident in the lives of countless believers
who have experienced healing in the name of Jesus, and in the
ministries of countless others who have allowed God to use them in
acts of healing, great and small.

It may be misleading to speak of a "revival" of Christian healing.
Christians have always prayed for healing; they have always been
used for healing even though they did not expect or understand
such things. What is relatively new today is that the idea of
healing is finding a more fertile cultural soil than in the past and is
reaching a broader audience of people aware of their own need for
healing and willing to trust in God's will for their wholeness.
Perhaps the best parts of the church's story of healing are yet to be
told.

Beyond the Stereotypes

Since beginning the journey of the ministry of healing, we have
seen many people healed or helped through the laying on of hands
and other types of prayer. In our experience, although God deals
with each person uniquely (and often in surprising ways), certain
patterns emerge again and again.

• Very often people are healed holistically, in a way that involves
every level of their being: body, mind, spirit, and emotions.
Sometimes healing even extends to events and circumstances that
impinge on persons' lives. For example, when Tilda becomes aware
of a need for personal healing in a certain area, often someone
comes into her office concerned about the same thing. In helping
the other person, Tilda is often helped herself.
• Although healing may not happen instantly, after prayer it
frequently occurs faster than might be predicted by medical
science.
• Healing usually results in an increased knowledge of the love of
God, a knowledge that is personal and experiential and leads to
joy. Most people, in addition, find a great freedom to stretch out
their hands to others as lovers and healers in the name of Jesus.

An illustration of the surprising and wholistic way God works with people is the story of Mary, a first-grade teacher and Roman Catholic nun for over forty years. Her beautiful story points to the way God often works with people.

Mary's Story

Mary had developed very painful ankles. The pain was so great that she found it difficult to teach. Her doctors were not certain if she suffered from a form of arthritis, and they were not able to help her very much.

Mary's predicament deeply troubled her. She loved teaching and considered it the ministry to which she was called. Her distress was compounded by her painful shyness. What could she do when she wasn't able to be with her "little people," the only ones with whom she was really comfortable?

When her suffering became evident to some members of her parish, they invited Mary to attend a healing prayer group in her church. She didn't want to go. She feared she might have to talk. Worse yet, if the parishioners prayed for her, she would be the center of attention. And then there were all those hands to touch her . . .

In the end, her friends won out. She went to the meeting and, as she suspected, found herself in the middle of a group of people. They prayed for her, their hands on her ankles: "Jesus, please heal Sister Mary's ankles . . . Hear our prayer, O God."

God heard; but God did not heal Mary's ankles.

As they prayed for healing of her ankles, her *ear* that had been nearly deaf since childhood suddenly opened; she could hear again. Amid the laughter and the tears that followed, any illusions that the group could predict with certainty what God would do melted away.

The next week Mary didn't need urging to attend the healing group. Once again they prayed for her ankles, and once again she experienced healing, but not in her ankles. Instead, the arthritis in her arm improved a little.

This went on week after week for several months. Each time the group prayed for Mary's ankles, some other minor ache or pain would vanish or at least feel better. Many times the group would end in laughter at the peculiar way God seemed to be working. However, Mary was certain that God was indeed at work, and the small physical improvements kept her coming back.

During this process, God was working marvelously with Mary in other ways. She became deeply aware that God loved her. Although in her mind Mary already knew this and had taught her first graders that "God is love," emotionally God had been to her like her own stern father. Now for the first time in her life, Mary felt the passionate, tender love of God for her. God was no longer a demanding parent ready with punishments if she didn't work very hard to please, but a father who delighted in her. Jesus became more real to her as a friend as well as a savior. Gradually Mary's shyness diminished, and she found she could read the Old Testament lesson at Sunday worship in front of hundreds of people, something she would not even have dreamed of doing only a few months before.

But guess what? She still had painful ankles. They had improved only a little after months of prayer.

Tilda asked Mary one day why she thought the pain in her ankles persisted. She replied: "My ankles were the bait that enticed me to pray for healing in the first place. The continued pain kept me coming back so that God could heal me in ways I didn't even know to pray for. I couldn't have imagined the depth of this healing and how it involved so much of me. Just think of what I would have missed if my ankles had been healed that first night. God had something much more profound in mind for me than just my ankles."

Then her eyes twinkled, and she smiled her wonderful smile. "Anyway, don't say my ankles weren't healed. Just say they aren't healed yet." Then she went on to say that she had begun to feel a new call to be a chaplain to some of the older sisters in her community who were in poor health. She was looking forward to developing a new ministry in this direction.

Mary's story points to some important truths about Christian healing, what it is and what it is not.

What Christian healing is NOT:

• Christian healing is not magic. It is not manipulating God to do what we want, but it is surrendering to God's healing work in us.
• Christian faith for healing is not a prediction of what God will do, but it is simple trust that God loves us and is at work in us already.
• Christian healing is not to be sought as a spiritual thrill for the healer or the person healed, but it is a way to grow as a Christian.
• Christian healing is not proof of our faith or holiness but is a sign of God's love.

What Christian healing is:

> *Christian healing is a process that involves the totality of our being—body, mind, emotion, spirit, and our social context—and that directs us toward becoming the person God is calling us to be at every stage of our living and our dying. Whenever we are truly open to God, some kind of healing takes place, because God yearns to bring us to wholeness. Through prayer and the laying on of hands, through confession, anointing, the sacraments, and other means of grace, Jesus meets us in our brokenness and pain and there loves, transforms, forgives, redeems, resurrects, and heals. Jesus does this in God's way, in God's time, and according to God's loving purpose for each person.*
>
> *Because the Holy Spirit is continually at work in each of us, pushing us toward wholeness, the process of healing is like removing sticks and leaves from a stream until the water runs clear. If we simply get out of the way of the Lord's work in us, we can trust that we are being led to the particular kind of wholeness God wills for us.*
>
> *Very often the results of our healing are increased faith in God and a new empowerment to love and serve others. Frequently we find that the very thing that caused our greatest brokenness becomes transformed into our own unique giftedness.*

In subsequent chapters we will recall this description of healing. Much of what follows will explain and illustrate the description.

Chapter 2

The Most Frequently Asked Questions About Healing

In our journeys in healing, we have learned the importance of asking questions. Both within ourselves and in the people with whom we work, questions inevitably arise. How could it be otherwise in an area as personal and sometimes as controversial as healing prayer? We have learned, too, that when questions are taken seriously they can lead to deep understanding and commitment. The questions raised in this chapter are the ones we hear most frequently. They are also the ones we ourselves have often asked and continue to ask. But before considering them let's examine the nature of questioning.

Honest questions are important because they can lead to deeper engagement. In all areas of Christian faith and life, questions are an important part of a thoughtful and growing faith. Often the more serious and seemingly radical the question, the greater its potential for leading to deep and life-changing insight. And what is true of the life of faith in general is especially true of healing prayer. The Spirit can use our questions and our doubts to lead us into deeper understandings of the healing process.

We occasionally encounter people, however, who ask lots of questions—often very good ones—as a defense against taking healing prayer seriously and personally. *Questions can be used as an avoidance mechanism, to block serious engagement.* This chapter identifies and deals with certain questions that could become blocking questions. After tackling these, questioners may feel freer to pursue what Christian healing means for them.

Preview of the Questions

QUESTIONS ARISING FROM A MODERN, SCIENTIFIC ORIENTATION

1. Isn't nonmedical healing just a result of the power of suggestion, that is, an example of the placebo effect?
2. Can you prove it? Can you say for sure that prayer or supernatural intervention effected a specific healing?
3. Shouldn't we put our trust in modern medicine? Isn't it dangerous to suggest that people can get along without medical science?

QUESTIONS ARISING FROM RESIGNATION TO GOD'S WILL OR TO "FATE"

4. Should we presume to tamper with nature by praying for healing, since disease and death are natural?
5. Shouldn't we pray that God's will be done and leave it at that? Isn't praying for anything more presumptuous?
6. Isn't it true that healing was for biblical times but not for now?

QUESTIONS ABOUT WHAT PRAYER IS AND IS NOT

7. Aren't we flirting with magic when we link human prayer with divine action in a cause-and-effect way?
8. If God wants to heal, why can't God just do it? Why are our prayers necessary?

SOCIAL AND ETHICAL RESERVATIONS ABOUT HEALING PRAYER

9. Isn't it selfish to pray for myself since other people are so much worse off?
10. Isn't an emphasis on healing narcissistic, just a form of religion suited to the "me generation"?
11. Isn't the focus on healing too individualistic, separating people from community and diverting them from social responsibility?

A QUESTION MASKING TIMIDITY, FEAR, OR
RESIGNATION

12. Why pray for healing? I tried it and it didn't work. When your
    time comes, it comes.

QUESTIONS ABOUT THE THEORY AND PRACTICE OF
HEALING PRAYER, ESPECIALLY THE PLACE OF FAITH IN
HEALING

13. Does a person have to have faith to be healed? Some seem to
    be healed without it.
14. Why don't some people get healed?
15. What if I pray, and healing doesn't happen? Is it because I'm a
    bad person or don't have enough faith?
16. What if I pray for another's healing and the person isn't
    healed? Couldn't this make him or her feel unworthy or
    abandoned by God? I don't want to "blame the victim."
17. Does a person need a special gift of healing in order to pray
    effectively for healing?

The questions are grouped by theme, with some inevitable
overlapping. It would scarcely be possible in a few sentences to
provide complete answers to these questions. Take the answers that
follow as jumping-off points for your own reflections. As you read,
reframe questions in your own terms, that is, "own" them. Also
make note of your own questions that are not included in the list.

Questions Arising from a Modern, Scientific Orientation

1. *Isn't non-medical healing just a result of the power of suggestion,
   that is, an example of the placebo effect?*

There is no doubt that the power of suggestion is very great in
the area of healing, as it is in other areas of human experience.
Most of us respond physically to positive, personal suggestion. We
can ease head and backaches by the power of positive thoughts or
positive imaging. Many of us can tell dramatic stories about the
effects of positive suggestion upon serious illness. The placebo
effect is real. In our day people are increasingly aware of body-mind

connections, the power of the mind to affect the body.[1] This is all to the good and fully in keeping with Christian faith. In fact, this intimate body-mind connection shows us that a strictly materialistic account of human life is very limited.

However, it is erroneous to try to explain away inner human experience, such as experiences of healing, as "merely" psychological. Trying to reduce religious experience to psychological terms impoverishes religious faith. For one thing, we as Christians affirm that God works through human psychological processes. To say healing is merely psychological, as if our minds and emotions were not a realm of divine activity, implies a limitation upon God. More than that, we affirm that *God does work* with people for their good. When we begin to act on that faith, our thinking shifts from "explaining God away" toward affirming God's healing activity in us.

2. *Can you prove it? Can you say for sure that prayer or supernatural intervention effected a specific healing?*

When we are talking about healing we are not dealing with the realm of empirical proof. By hard scientific standards, probably most of the evidence for healing is anecdotal (but what anecdotes!). However, we affirm the importance of those areas of life that are not subject to proof, where the human element is paramount. Those areas include human values, personal relations, and religious experience.

While not devaluing science and technology, we recognize that an exclusively scientific mindset can block positive experiences of healing prayer. We suggest to the skeptics that they lay their skepticism aside for a while—imagine putting it on a shelf where it can be retrieved later—so that another way of experiencing reality, another way of knowing, may be allowed to come to the fore.

3. *Shouldn't we put our trust in modern medicine? Isn't it dangerous to suggest that people can get along without medical science?*

Healing prayer is *not* an alternative to medical care. Grounded in the incarnation, *Christian faith affirms that the art and science of medicine is a good gift of God and is one of the ways God heals.* Those forms of healing that make a test of faith out of giving up medicine are based on a theology that, we believe, artificially separates the mind and spirit from the body.

But the important question is, should Christians trust in modern medicine alone? Put that way, of course Christians should not trust in anything, *alone*, other than God! Trusting in God the healer, then, means employing all the means of healing God has provided: good physical and mental self-care, medical science, *and* the spiritual means of healing given in the Christian tradition—prayer, laying on of hands and anointing, public worship, and the sacraments. How strange it would seem for Christians not to draw on all the means of healing God provides!

Behind these first three questions lies a skepticism about whether God really acts in the world. Such skepticism is deeply ingrained in the modern worldview and affects most Westerners, religious and nonreligious alike. The theological and philosophical issues are highly complex. But *a strictly scientific approach to healing is broadened and enriched when we acknowledge three things.* First, modern science itself advocates a much more open view of reality, including the interpenetration of the physical and nonphysical, than laypersons in science usually realize.[2] Christians who continue to think in terms of a sharp separation of body and mind are actually lagging behind their secular counterparts! Second, some contemporary models of Christian theology are breaking down the dualism of earlier times. These provide resources for a solid theological grounding for the practice of healing prayer.[3] Third, and most important, *the practice of healing prayer will always be something experienced before it is understood, known by the heart before it is grasped by the mind.* The concerns of the scientific worldview, legitimate and appropriate in themselves, need not become blocks to exploring healing prayer. What are needed for that journey are an open mind and heart and a trust in God our good creator and healer.

Questions Arising from Resignation to God's Will or to "Fate"

4. *Should we presume to tamper with nature by praying for healing, since disease and death are natural?*

Death is indeed entirely natural. Death can even be seen as a kindly part of the larger cycle of life. We know, too, that death can be the ultimate healing for persons who have suffered long, wasting illnesses. Hospital chaplains sometimes see well-meant prayers for a loved one's healing stand in the way of the release that comes with the suffering person's timely death. Surrendering him or her to God's care and love might assist the process toward a peaceful death. Always, wisdom and discernment are needed to help us know what to pray for and how to pray in a given situation. None of this means that we ought not to pray for healing, only that we ought to bring into our prayers an openness to God's loving will, which is infinitely wiser and more perfect than ours. Jesus said, "If you then, who are evil, know how to give good gifts to your children, how much more will your Father [Parent] who is in heaven give good things to those who ask [Matt. 7:11]?" These words assure us that God does want us to be whole and that God can be trusted to bestow the kind of healing that is right for the moment, even if it be the healing of death.

5. *Shouldn't we pray that God's will be done and leave it at that? Isn't praying for anything more presumptuous?*

There is a kind of religious fatalism, a stoic submission to the implacable will of God, that is deeply ingrained in our heritage. Although this attitude appears to be genuinely "faithful" and may truly be so, it needs to be examined carefully.

When our ancestors buried their dead, so often untimely taken, they might console themselves with the words of Job: "The Lord gave, and the Lord has taken away; blessed be the name of the Lord [Job 1:21]." They were tapping into a strain of biblical faith that saw Yahweh's hand alike in health and illness, healing and death. "I kill and I make alive; I wound and I heal; and there is none that can deliver out of my hand [Deut. 32:39]."4 It is not surprising that many of us, expecially in times of personal tragedy, resort to this faithful-sounding fatalism. It can be a way of trying to make sense of what may otherwise seem inexplicably tragic.

But there are other strains in the biblical tradition that highlight God's love as the source of healing and wholeness. Recall Yahweh's promise to Israel at the outset of the wilderness wandering: "I am the Lord, your healer [Exod. 15:26]." The prophet Elijah's miraculous raising of the widow's son is of this sort (1 Kings 17:17–24), as is Elisha's raising of the Shunammite woman's son (2 Kings 4:18–37).[5] The Gospels portray Jesus healing all manner of illness. The assumption is that Jesus' healings are in accord with God's will. Often in Jesus' healings, those who come or are brought for healing have demonstrated their great desire and need for healing. Jesus receives and honors their desire and responds as we believe God responds, by meeting their needs and granting their requests.

Jesus' own prayer in Gethsemane perfectly epitomizes the faithful attitude: "Father, all things are possible to thee; remove this cup from me; yet, not what I will, but what thou wilt [Mark 14:36]."[6] Jesus felt free to ask for his heart's desire; he was also ready to give over his own wish to the will of God. *There is a great difference between two kinds of surrender—giving up and giving over.* Fatalism is giving up. In contrast, in our praying we do not pretend to impose our wills upon God; rather, we seek to *give* ourselves *over* to what God wants to do in and through us. Such an attitude honors God's will above all but is not fatalistic.

6. Isn't it true that healing was for biblical times but not for now?

This view has been traditionally held by some fundamentalist Christians who believe history is divided into dispensations, or epochs.[7] In this view, miracles are associated with the dispensation of the founding of the church but are not part of God's work today. Recently, the number of people espousing this belief has declined considerably, though some Christians still hold to it.

The dispensationists' view on healing is mistaken for two reasons. First, it is not biblical. Nowhere in the Bible is the phenomenon of healing limited to a particular time. On the contrary, the Bible gives the strong impression that part of God's unchanging character is to desire wholeness for every creature. Confident of that, we pray for healing.

Second, God continues to heal, despite dispensationalism! Healing has been a part of the historic church's ministry since the close of the apostolic age.[8] Also, we are experiencing a resurgence of healing prayer in our day. Among charismatics and mainstream believers, high-church Episcopalians and low-church Mennonites, pietists and activists, more and more people are finding encouragement to pray for healing. Healing is most assuredly for today.

Questions About What Prayer Is and Is Not

7. *Aren't we flirting with magic when we link human prayer with divine action in a cause-and-effect way?*

Magic is the human attempt to affect, or coerce, supernatural forces by natural means, as when a charm is worn to ward off evil spirits. It has little to do with what we understand about prayer as Jesus modeled it and as practiced by the saints of the church. In praying for healing, we don't imagine we are coercing the divine will, or directing God, or informing God of things God would otherwise not have known.

Prayer is not directing God but directing ourselves toward God; not informing God but conforming to God. Assisted by the Holy Spirit, in prayer we listen to God in the faith that we may receive and channel God's limitless love. Healing prayer, then, is a matter of discerning how God wants to heal and of praying for that. This is not magic, but it is a mystery—the mystery of entering into communion with God through the Holy Spirit.

8. *If God wants to heal, why can't God just do it? Why are our prayers necessary?*

Sometimes it appears that God works quite independently of any known human prayer or intercession. Once we open our eyes to God's healing activity, we can expect to be utterly surprised at the things that happen. At such times we conclude that there doesn't seem to be anything God cannot do. More often, perhaps, our experience is of God's self-limiting, that is, of God's honoring human freedom and waiting upon our responses to grace. Each of us will resolve the theological issues differently. But the experience of healing ministry is that God desires our prayers and does sometimes seem to wait for our prayers. It doesn't seem right to insist that our prayers are necessary, for that would be to limit God. It does seem right to respond to the divine invitation to pray for healing, trusting that God will use these prayers for good in ways we may or may not fully grasp. In short, we pray out of obedience to the call to pray.

Social and Ethical Reservations About Healing Prayer

9. *Isn't it selfish to pray for myself since other people are so much worse off?*

It may sound altruistic, even heroic, when someone in dire need asks this. We may be tempted to admire their selflessness. But fear of being selfish can be a cop-out from taking care of ourselves or responsibility for ourselves. It may even mask unresolved feelings of unworthiness or guilt. Perhaps we feel there is a part of us unworthy of God's love. But how can it be selfish to value ourselves even as God values us? It is this *appropriate self-regard* that motivates us to ask God to make us the whole persons we are intended to be. Also, however we feel about ourselves, praying for our own healing responds to a call from God to be on the journey toward wholeness.

10. *Isn't an emphasis on healing narcissistic, just a form of religion suited to the "me generation"?*

Narcissus was the beautiful youth who fell in love with his own image. Intense self-involvement is undoubtedly a mark of our culture, and it is an activity Christians need to resist. During illness there is a natural tendency to become somewhat self-absorbed, and an emphasis upon healing could play upon and heighten narcissism. It could cause the one needing healing to become extremely self-involved. (Unfortunately, some forms of healing ministry seems to evoke this attitude.)

However, desiring to be healed need not be narcissistic when healing is seen as growing toward the whole person God intends us to be. Focusing on *God's* will for us should help us distinguish between appropriate and inappropriate self-love.

11. *Isn't the focus on healing too individualistic, separating people from community and diverting them from social responsibility?*

Reflecting the individualism of contemporary American culture, some expressions of healing, whether New Age or television faith-healing, do seem to focus upon individual healing as an end in itself. Some persons who are involved in healing show little concern for anything beyond themselves. Most healing services and most books about healing make no mention of the social dimensions of human life.

Is it inevitable that healing ministries and justice ministries must go their separate ways? Are these not simply two alternative versions of the faith? These are crucial questions, especially for the mainstream church today. Our conviction, however, is strong. No understanding of healing prayer is adequate that takes individuals out of community or that separates individual wholeness from social wholeness. To put the matter positively, *the church's healing ministry should always address both the social order and the lives of individuals; authentic Christian healing will be both social and individual in its impact.* 9

This point of view is rooted in several convictions. First, Jesus healed not simply because he felt compassion for individuals, though he surely was compassionate (see Mark 1:41; 8:2). He healed because he thereby brought the rule of God—that is, the active power and presence of God—into the lives of the people as a whole. As with Jesus' healing ministry, so also with the church's healing ministry today. Beyond the love and compassion we naturally feel for those who suffer, we pray especially for healing because we believe that God will use our prayers to establish the divine rule, not only within individuals, but also within the church and upon all creation. One of the things that makes Christian healing "Christian" is just this corporate framework of God's healing work. From this point of view, there can be no exclusive focus upon individual healing.

Second, the more we grow toward wholeness, the more we will be sensitized to the needs of the world around us and equipped for doing God's will and work in the world. Healing of the body or mind that did not issue in a deeper commitment to peace and justice would be only partial at best.

Third, we are called to pray not just for the healing of individuals but for the healing of the social order. To put the matter more strongly, encountering social evil (the modern-day social equivalent of Jesus' casting out demons) is a part of the church's healing ministry.[10]

In short, we need to overcome the false and misleading separation sometimes made between the individually spiritualized and the social activist forms of faith. In Christian healing such a separation may sometimes be encountered in practice but needs to be transcended.

A Question Masking Timidity, Fear, or Resignation

12. *Why pray for healing? I tried it and it didn't work. When your time comes, it comes.*

Questions and statements such as these may express many attitudes and emotions. Sometimes they can be used as excuses for not opening up to the possibility of healing. Strange as it may seem, sometimes people prefer the limitation or illness they know to the unknown changes healing would bring. Jesus' question to the man paralyzed thirty-eight years is pertinent: "Do you want to be well [John 5:6]?" Sometimes people give up, resigning themselves to their afflictions or limitations. Thus they relinquish the initiative to act in their own behalf or even to let the Spirit intercede for them (Romans 8:26). In such cases we are dealing not with rational challenges to the idea of healing but with faintheartedness or fear. The appropriate response, then, is to kindle or rekindle trust in God the healer, who desires wholeness and is able to heal.

Sometimes a feeling of resignation arises out of the mistaken idea that healing should come virtually instantaneously in response to a single prayer of faith, as for example from the person who attends one healing service to cure a serious malady. When healing doesn't happen quickly, the person loses interest in the process. Hence the timid conclusion, "I tried it and it didn't work." But recall the definition of healing in chapter 1: healing is a *process*. True, sometimes the process can be very fast, practically instantaneous! But that is not the usual experience. Also, if we were to stop praying after one, two, or three prayers, we could be cutting ourselves off from what God wants to do in our lives. One-time "faith healing" is not comparable to the process of healing inaugurated when we open ourselves to the ongoing activity of the Holy Spirit.

Questions About the Theory and Practice of Healing Prayer, Especially the Place of Faith in Healing

13. *Does a person have to have faith to be healed? Some seem to be healed without it.*

The short answer to this question is no. Faith—whether faith in Jesus Christ or a more general religious faith—is not a prerequisite for healing. That is, God can get around our lack of faith. But a longer answer is required, because few issues are as troublesome in theory and practice as the relation of faith to healing.

In the movement popularly known as faith healing—a term not used in this book to describe healing prayer—a harmful, unethical, and false logic is employed:

If you have enough faith, you will be healed; therefore, if you aren't healed, it's because you don't have enough faith.

This simplistic formula is harmful because it "blames the victim" for any apparent failure to be healed, adding guilt to the sufferer's burdens. The formula is also unethical. The "healer" who employs it is often surrounded with an aura of power and holiness. If healing doesn't happen, all the blame falls on the one seeking healing; the healer is immune from scrutiny. It is not surprising that people in this position are sometimes tempted to abuse their gifts.

We believe the faith-healing formula is also theologically wrong. It appears to coerce God, to say, "If I have enough faith, then God *must* do what I want." Such an idea borders on magic. Also, it expresses an inadequate understanding of what faith is in the biblical sense. What is enough faith? Is faith something quantifiable? *Biblical faith is more a matter of trusting in Jesus' power and God's love than believing that a certain result will be achieved.* Yes, we can have "little" faith or "great" faith (see Matthew 14:31; 15:28), but that is more a measure of the *quality and completeness of our dependence upon God* than of what or how much we believe.

Finally, the faith-healing formula tends wrongly to shift the focus to *my* believing rather than to the One whom I trust. Faith then becomes "faith in faith" rather than "faith in God."[11] (While we have identified this linkage of faith and healing with the movement called faith healing, in fact this way of thinking occurs quite commonly, especially when people are under the stress of serious illness.)

Let us now explore the question of the relation of faith and healing from the perspective of the words and deeds of Jesus in the Gospels. There we find material that both challenges and confirms our approach.

The most challenging biblical material is a series of Jesus' sayings that express a very radical and positive link between faith and answered prayer. Consider these:

> "For truly, I say to you, if you have faith as a grain of mustard seed, you will say to this mountain, 'Move hence to yonder place,' and it will move; and nothing will be impossible to you."
> —Matthew 17:20; see also Luke 17:5

> And Jesus answered them, "Have faith in God. Truly, I say to you, whoever says to this mountain, 'Be taken up and cast into the sea,' and does not doubt in his heart, but believes that what he says will come to pass, it will be done for him. Therefore I tell you, whatever you ask in prayer, believe that you receive it, and you will."
> —Mark 11:22–24;
> see also Matthew 17:14–21; Luke 9:37–43

> "Whatever you ask in my name, I will do it, that the Father may be glorified in the Son; if you ask anything in my name, I will do it."
> —John 14:13–14[12]

In addition, faith is mentioned as a factor in healing in seven of the eighteen separate healing miracles of the Gospels (excluding parallel accounts). For example, three times Jesus says, "Your faith has healed you," or "Be it done according to your faith," or similar words (Mark 5:34; 10:52; Luke 17:19; Matthew 9:29; see also Matthew 8:10, 13; Mark 2:5; 5:36).

Faith is named as a factor in two of the five separate accounts of Jesus casting out demons. He says to the Canaanite woman who pleads on behalf of her daughter, "O woman, great is your faith! Be it done for you as you desire [Matt. 15:28; but compare Mark 7:28–29]." And to the father who says on behalf of his son, "If you can do anything, have pity on us and help us," Jesus replies, "If you can! All things are possible to one who believes [Mark 9:22–23]."[13]

What are we to make of this evidence? Clearly Jesus spoke with astonishing boldness about what God is able to do through people who trust in God utterly. Nevertheless, it would be a mistake to turn these sayings into a rigid faith-healing system. First, we should recognize that hyperbole, or exaggerated speech, was a characteristic trait of Jesus' speech. Remember the camel and the needle's eye, and the threat of hell for calling someone a fool (Matthew 19:24; 5:22). Such sayings were not meant to be taken literally, as spiritual laws. Hyperbole was a device whereby Jesus seized his hearers' imaginations and pierced their defenses.[14]

Second, we should also recognize that these bold utterances ought not be lifted out as proof texts, that is, taken in isolation from the whole biblical message about the interaction of divine power and human freedom. Again and again in scripture we encounter poignant stories of people of great faith who endured much suffering and did not receive specific healings.[15]

The harm and error of the faith-healing formula is tragically illustrated by the story of a deeply disturbed man who, on his twelfth suicide attempt, lost a leg when he threw himself in the path of a train. He survived somehow but during his recovery was persuaded by a faith healer that God could grow his leg back if he just had enough faith. To a man already deeply depressed and mentally unstable, this approach simply wreaked further emotional havoc.

Recognizing the limits and conditions to these bold sayings of Jesus, we may still allow ourselves to be moved to greater boldness of faith and expectation than we usually have. We would then take these sayings seriously and faithfully, without making of them a simplistic formula of faith healing.

It is important to note that *about two-thirds of the Gospel healing and deliverance stories lack any mention of faith.* Probably some of the people healed came to Jesus with confidence in him, like the leper who knelt before Jesus and said, "If you will, you can make me clean [Mark 1:40]." Often, however, those whom Jesus healed were not people of faith but just happened to be in the right place at the right time, like the man in the synagogue (Mark 1:23 ff.), or the man beside the pool (John 5:2–9), or the man born blind who didn't even know who Jesus was (John 9). This broader survey of Jesus' healings is evidence that the faith-healing formula is not justified on biblical grounds.

Faith, we conclude, understood as reliance upon God and trust in Jesus the healer, is profoundly important in healing prayer, as it is in every aspect of our lives. We never cease needing to become bolder and more radical in our reliance upon God. But to insist on the strict connection between healing and faith is not consistent with the stories of Jesus' healings. It is also not good theology, good ethics, or good pastoral care to perpetuate the faith-healing formula. Experience in healing ministry supports the view that God can get around our little faith.

14. *Why don't some people get healed?*[16]

We have already expressed the belief that any time a person truly opens herself or himself to God, *some healing always takes place,* even though perhaps not in the way we might expect. But just as there are factors that contribute to "an environment conducive to healing," there are factors that inhibit or detract from healing.[17] Perhaps the people who pray have not accurately discerned how or what to pray for.[18] Or the one needing healing may be blocking the work of the Spirit in any number of ways—by holding onto resentment or being unwilling to forgive, or by secretly preferring to stay with the familiar suffering, or by continuing an unhealthy lifestyle that has caused the illness. Also perhaps the time is not right, as well as the people, in order to effect the healing that seems to be needed.[19]

Most important to these inquiries is the fact that healing is a mystery, even as God's way with each of us is a mystery. An exhaustive answer to the question of why people are not healed can never be given. While affirming God's disposition to bless us always, we recognize that there are important factors that may inhibit the healing process. When we discover in ourselves or in others the presence of such a factor, then we can focus on that factor in our prayers.

15. *What if I pray, and healing doesn't happen? Is it because I'm a bad person or don't have enough faith?*

This is the personal and existential form of the last question. Hospital chaplains and pastoral counselors can attest to the common human tendency to find a reason, or a scapegoat, for illness and for the apparent failure of healing prayer. Many religious people in particular voice feelings of guilt or low self-esteem under the stress of suffering and illness.

The feeling that one is a bad person whose unanswered prayers are God's punishment is itself a crippling emotional condition that calls out for healing prayer. To be freed of such personal judgment and to accept God's unconditional love is one of the greatest forms of healing anyone can receive.

Do illness and the withholding of healing express divine punishment for being a "bad person"? Put that way, the answer is clear: We do not believe illness is a punishment from God, nor do we believe God withholds healing in order to punish sin. Neither an individual's tumor, nor chronic depression, nor AIDS, nor any disease is sent by God or perpetuated by God as punishment. Although there are Hebrew scripture texts that speak of both healing and illness as sent by God and of illness being brought on by sin,[20] they are not the major thrust of biblical faith about illness, especially as seen in the words and deeds of Jesus. Jesus refused to speculate on the cause of illness or other bad things (see John 9:2–3; Luke 13:1–5). What he did instead was simply to touch the sick and heal them of their diseases and in that way embody the compassion of God.

Finally, we need to remind ourselves to let God set the healing agenda, not presume to know what needs to happen or what healing will look like in a specific instance. Also, we need to emphasize good pastoral discernment in framing our prayers for healing, discernment sensitive to the movement of the Spirit and to the dynamics manifested in each healing situation.

16. *What if I pray for another's healing and the person isn't healed? Couldn't this make him or her feel unworthy or abandoned by God? I don't want to "blame the victim."*

There is good, caring motivation behind this question. Just as medical caregivers want above all to avoid doing harm to their patients, so those praying for others do not want the person's condition to worsen by glibly creating hopes that are not fulfilled. Many sensitive pastors hesitate to pray for healing because they do not want to create unfulfilled hopes in people who are already hurting. Such responsible pastoral concern is valid and commendable. However, healing prayer cannot harm and, in fact, richly contributes to good pastoral care when we keep these things in mind:

- God wants people to be whole, and some kind of healing takes place when people open themselves to the Spirit;
- God, not we, sets the healing agenda; we may not know what healing will look like in a given case;
- Our first task is to discern what to pray for and how to pray.

17. *Does a person need a special gift of healing in order to pray effectively for healing?*

The apostle Paul names gifts of healing among the spiritual gifts given to certain people for the common good (1 Corinthians 12:9). In the church today, there do seem to be people with special gifts—whether we think of them as talents, sensitivities, or spiritual gifts—in healing prayer. Such people should be encouraged to discover, own, and cultivate their gifts. It is important for these gifts to be confirmed within the community of faith.

Most of us, however, probably do not have extraordinary gifts of healing, but we do have a role in healing prayer. Francis MacNutt has said that healing is like music. Although we are not all a Mozart, we can all play an instrument and improve with practice!

The gift of healing is not a private possession, in any case. As Jesus sent forth his disciples to preach and heal and cast out demons, not designating specialists but giving the tasks to all, so *churches today are called and gifted to become healing communities. The gift of healing is given to the whole body of Christ, to be exercised by all the members of the body.* [21] What this means practically is that each member of the faith community should be encouraged to practice praying for healing and can learn to pray in ways that are personally comfortable and meaningful within the community. For some this may be nothing more dramatic than silently praying for others at home or in the church pew; for others it may mean joining a prayer circle or a healing team that visits the sick. What is important is that we catch a vision of the church as a healing community and begin to contribute to that community.

Conclusion

We have worked through a crucial and possibly daunting list of questions! Even so, we may not have touched upon your personal, most urgent concerns. Questions about healing prayer, whatever they may be, are important and valid. Although we cannot have answered these questions fully here, you now have a perspective and a starting point for further work. Continue questioning to deepen and enrich the process of exploring healing prayer.

Chapter 3

Praying for the Person God Is Calling Me to Be

A woman named Lois prays every day that God will "grow" her. Recently, Lois' alcoholic father died after a long illness. She had taken care of him for several years until the end.

Early in her father's illness, Lois became aware of her rage toward her father. When she was small, he hadn't been much of a father and, as he got older, his addiction became more and more central to his life. As her anger bubbled to the surface, she felt led to express it and, later, to let go of it. She did not tell her dying father much about her built-up anger. Instead, she wrote it in her journal, painted it, and beat up pillows. She sobbed and yelled her anger to her therapist. She felt it deeply and allowed its expression.

Then one day she imagined Jesus asking that her anger be given to him. It seemed to her that she was carrying all her anger from her childhood gathered up in a house painter's drop cloth. In her prayerful imagination she handed the large parcel to Jesus, who accepted it and threw it away. She felt freer and lighter than she had in months, truly rid of the anger that had poisoned her life.

Some time after this, she "heard" as she prayed that she should tell her father that she loved him. Words of love had been said very rarely as Lois was growing up, and it was not easy for her now. She tried for months to get the words out, but they seemed stuck in her throat. She asked God to help her do this difficult thing, but nothing happened right away.

One day Lois's cat was hit by a car. Holding her mortally wounded pet, Lois sank down on the floor and sobbed. Her father

34

sat by silently. This was an opportunity, and Lois decided to use it. She blurted out: "Pop, you see how much I'm crying now? Well, when you die I'm going to cry even harder." Then the words she had been trying to say for so long just came tumbling out. "I love you, Pop." He didn't respond, but she knew he heard. After that, it was easier to say "Daddy, I love you."

As she said the words over and over, her own capacity to love and forgive grew rapidly. She found herself tenderly loving and forgiving this old man who had hurt her so deeply as a child and who could not or would not return her caring words and deeds. She was able to give up her need to have him love her in a particular way. In the process she grew to be a little bit more like Jesus. Also, she was more at peace, more joyful, and less physically tense. She was able to say good-bye when her father died, and she freely cried out her grief.

A few months after her father's death, Lois felt a renewed call to work with persons with AIDS. Her experience with her father was being turned into a gift to work with others who were dying. Lois was healed, not in the sense of arriving somehow at a state of perfect health, but in the sense of being gently led and companioned on a healing journey toward wholeness in mind, body, emotions, and spirit.

Some people find it easier to pray for others than to pray for themselves. However, the more we pray for the brokenness and pain of other people, the more we are made aware of our own need for healing. With growing sensitivity, we will see ourselves in many of the people for whom we pray. We know we are indeed wounded healers. If we are open, we will sense God's invitation to allow us to grow toward wholeness just as Lois did.

Lois' story illustrates many of the points in the definition of Christian healing found on page 15. Following is a review of the key phrases.

God's Desire for Human Wholeness

God desires our health, our wholeness of body, mind, and spirit. We read throughout the Bible how God yearned for and brooded over Israel, making a covenant and sending prophets to bring the people to justice and righteousness. God's covenant relationship with Israel was understood as a call to personal and social wholeness, the biblical concept of *shalom*.

Jesus, the living, human expression of God, went about the countryside restoring people to health. He healed those with various diseases as if to say, "This is how much God loves you." The Gospel writers paint a picture of Jesus as one who was always ready to help those who were hurting.

Emphasizing God's desire for our wholeness is sure to raise a serious and challenging question: If God desires our healing so much, why isn't everyone healed?"[1] Why do people suffer terribly? Why do innocent children die? Why does God allow ruthless and greedy people to come out on top? And if the questioner is personally involved, the question becomes powerful indeed: Why did my husband die at age thirty-nine even though I prayed for his healing? This is the sort of problem that must be worked through on many levels. When God leads a seeker to a resolution of such a searing question, surely this has been the occasion for healing.

The question of suffering is one of the most difficult and persistant in all of Christian theology, and even a preliminary discussion of the issues is far more than we can deal with in this book.[2] Even the most profound thinkers on the subject acknowledge that the question of why suffering exists if God is loving and all-powerful ends with the infinite mystery of God's being.

This is not, however, to say that we should give up our pondering. One direction for thinking about suffering is that God seems to limit God's own power out of respect for human freedom. God did not create us to be robots—even holy robots. God has given us the awesome freedom to choose, and perhaps this is what makes us uniquely human. But freedom means that we can choose cruelty over love, greed and selfishness instead of generosity, neglect rather than responsibility and commitment. As a nation, we choose to spend money on instruments of war rather than on medical research or programs for the poor. We might even say that much suffering is caused by the choices made by human beings and does not reflect God's desire to make us suffer.[3]

Another line of thought is that much suffering is caused by the natural operation of the universe. In the natural world, accidents, earthquakes, and hurricanes occur; and eventually all living things must die. When suffering occurs as a result of these natural processes, it is no one's fault and not God's positive will, except in a secondary sense. God made the world to function as it does for our good, not to make us suffer.[4] We know that God's loving presence is with us, no matter what we go through. This is central to our faith.

Indeed, God invites us to ask for what we need just as a child would ask a parent. Our experience teaches us that whenever we open ourselves to the activity of the Holy Spirit, some kind of healing takes place, despite the power of destructive human choices and the operations of nature.

Discerning Who God Is Calling Me to Be

God not only yearns for our wholeness but is also actively involved in our growth. The wholeness offered to each person is unique and particular, rooted in God's will for each person. Each person's state of "health" is different, and healing will follow a different course. For example, one person who prays for physical healing is restored instantly, even as he or she prays. For another, physical healing takes longer. Often the healing process takes a person into realms of emotional healing before physical healing takes place. Sometimes physical healing is not given, but the person is healed in ways that make the physical illness a gift.

In addition, each person has a different personality and history. Whether you are fiery and energetic or serene and laid back, whether you have lived a tragic life or one of relative ease and happiness, God molds the material into your particular call to wholeness. The specifics of God's healing change over the course of a life as well. The healing agenda for a lonely teenager is different from that of a busy forty-two year-old, and still different for a person of great age preparing for death.[5]

These are some conclusions to draw from viewing healing as a unique process for each person:

- When we speak of healing, we do not necessarily mean perfect health, *but God's perfect will for us at each stage of our lives.*
- Healing prayer is not just for the times when we are sick or

troubled, but is for a *lifetime, a process of growth and maturation into the person God created us to be.*

• God's healing is not some sort of divine zap, which comes from outside. Instead it *engages every part of our being in response to and in cooperation with God's activity.*

• Christian healing prayer is a process of discovering what the Holy Spirit is bringing to birth in us and of praying for that. *It is the surrender to God's continuing creation in us.*

Discernment

The process of discovering God's will or the direction of the Holy Spirit is called discernment. While discernment is at the heart of healing prayer, it is not familiar to most mainstream Protestant Christians. It has, however, been a part of the church's wisdom throughout the ages. For example, Ignatius of Loyola, writing in the sixteenth century, spoke at great length about the discernment process in his classic, *The Spiritual Exercises.* [6] Similarly, modern spiritual directors seek to assist those they direct with discernment. Protestant pastors and laypeople are also becoming more focused on the process of discernment.

Despite the growing attention to discernment in the twentieth century, many people may still mistakenly think discernment means having absolutely certain knowledge of what God wants in a specific situation. They wonder how anyone can be "that" sure. They may well be turned off by Christians who punctuate every sentence with "God told me . . ." Or they may feel that, while some very saintly people know God's specific will, ordinary people will probably know God's will only in a general way. Thus, they feel the best they can do is to figure out a general direction from the Bible and the wisdom of the church, and add to that their own common sense.

In fact, appealing to scripture, tradition, and reason is surely part of any responsible discernment process. We can test the validity of what we perceive by asking ourselves: "Does this sound like the God of the Bible?" "Does it reflect the best thinking of the church?" "Does it seem sensible?" [7]

But there is more to discernment than inference, for discernment is rooted in the faith that God seeks to be in personal relationship with each of us. In this faith we believe that God does speak to us personally about our particular lives.

How does this happen in the life of a Christian? It happens through inviting God to speak and then listening—not for audible sounds from heaven—but for the still, small voice that speaks through what is going on around us and inside us.

God speaks in many different ways, and grace gives us the eyes to see and the ears to hear. For example, God may speak through pictures that form in our minds as we pray or in ideas that seem to float into our awareness. We may suddenly remember a verse from scripture, a hymn text, or something that happened long ago. In addition, God may speak in dreams,[8] or in events, or in words spoken by a friend. The important thing is to pray for the grace to know God's voice, to test it a bit, and then to act in faith on the discernment given, trusting that God will correct us if we haven't heard quite accurately.

Discerning, then, is not expecting "skywriting," God's telling us exactly what we need to know. It very seldom happens that way. Instead, in discerning we pray for grace to enter into an awareness of what God is communicating to us.[9]

Steps in a Discernment Process

How does one concretely enter into a discernment process? A brief description of the steps in such a process follows.

1. Tell God how you feel, as honestly as you can. Don't get pious about this. Take a lesson from the psalms. If you feel like choking someone with your bare hands, say so. If you doubt that God is paying attention, say that too. If you are depressed, confused, worried, sick of being sick, admit it. This step is very important, one often skipped by Christians who want to keep everything "nice."

2. Invite God into all of your brokenness. Ask God to heal you and to show you what to pray for.

3. Then stop talking—even in your head—and simply sit in God's presence, with the expectation that God will work in some way. Allow some time for this, say fifteen to twenty minutes.

4. Pay attention to what happens in the silence: What images,

thoughts, memories come to you? What physical sensations? What desires? What emerges as an action you should
take?

5. You might want to imagine Jesus with you. What does he
   say to you? What does he do? (This way of praying, called
   "faith imagination," will be discussed later in this chapter.)
6. It may be helpful to jot down very briefly whatever impres-
   sions come to you as you pray.
7. You may immediately see a pattern that suggests a direction
   for prayer. If so, act on this discernment by praying along
   the lines suggested.

For example, you pray about having the blahs. Nothing seems
exciting or interesting, and you feel tired all the time, even though
on the surface things seem to be going well. As you wait for God to
work, you see in your mind the face of a person who hurt you. You
remember what the person did and your reaction to it. *Trust that
this memory came up at this time for a reason and that it is somehow
related to the issue at hand.* After all, you asked God to work in you!
So, in response to your discernment, shift your focus from your
lack of energy to the image of the one who hurt you. Ask God to
help you release your anger and to forgive the person. Continue to
ask God for discernment about the steps you need to take in this
process.

If you are praying about the blahs and you get the notion to have
a physical examination, do it! Trust enough to act on whatever
leading you are given if your action is reasonable and consistent
with the God of the Bible.

Tilda tells this story of asking for discernment about her feeling
of the blahs.

> *Discernment came in the form of the following dream: A friend of
> mine who is a fine classical musician walked up to me and with great
> solemnity gazed into my eyes for several minutes. She didn't smile or
> blink, and I had the sense that something important was about to
> happen. Then gravely she asked me a very silly question: "Tilda,
> what if 'Inky Dinky Parley Voo' was really written by Bach?" Then
> she broke into delighted peals of laughter. I woke up laughing myself,
> and sensing that God had indeed answered my prayer. It seemed clear*

that I needed to lighten up, to see the humor even in "serious" things, to have fun, to be silly at times. As I prayed for the grace to do this, over the next few weeks, the plodding, gray fatigue that I had been experiencing gradually melted away.

8. If nothing occurs to you after you have asked God for discernment, don't be discouraged. Keep asking, and re-member that God speaks in many ways. Be open to God's voice and action in books you read, phone calls you receive, events in your life, and so on. Remember how powerfully God acted in the death of Lois's cat as Lois prayed to say to her father "I love you."

9. Trust that if your discernment is off the mark, the Holy Spirit will somehow correct you. Simply remain as open as possible and act in faith on whatever discernment you receive.

10. If your discernment process truly draws a blank, of course you can still pray. You might say: "Lord, I don't know how you want to heal me, but I know you are a God of love and compassion. Please heal me in the way that is best for me."

Pursuing the Call to Wholeness

Let us restate part of our definition of Christian healing: "Because the Holy Spirit is continually at work in each of us, pushing us toward wholeness, the process of healing is like removing sticks and leaves from a stream until the water runs clear. If we simply get out of the way of the Lord's work in us, we can trust that we are being led to the particular kind of wholeness God wills for us."

It sounds simple, doesn't it? All that we have to do is get out of the way of God's work in us and some kind of healing will flow. Yet we know it is not so simple. Taking the "sticks and leaves" away may be painful. With them gone we may feel afraid or uncomfort-able. Not accidentally Jesus asked the man waiting to be healed by the pool of Siloam, "Do you want to be healed [John 5:6]?" Like that man, many of us may find it hard to give up a way of life that feels familiar even though painful. We hang onto our suffering, often clutching painful memories, resentments, or guilt as though they were treasures.[10] Even physical suffering may have a payoff. Here is an example.

When Janet has the flu for a few days, she mostly doesn't enjoy being sick; she can't wait to feel better. But while she's sick, her husband and kids bring her tea and toast in bed. They screen her phone calls and make things as easy as possible for her. She has to admit that some very nice things accompany being sick.

A major illness may play out these responses on a large scale. Not that everyone with a major physical illness is actually a sneaky malingerer who enjoys being the center of attention. Far from it! But with suffering comes a healthy drive to make life more tolerable for ourselves. Sometimes we adapt so well to a life of illness and pain that we find it hard to let go of our adaptations when the time comes to be well.

For example, major illnesses have been known to cement a faltering relationship or provide the perfect reason for a person not to engage in a demanding task.[11] This can be true of emotional and spiritual pain as well. Someone once asked: "Who will I be if I give up my depression? I can't imagine being me and not being depressed. It's who I am."

One way to "clear the stream" is to ask ourselves and God whether we experience any payoff in our suffering. Are we holding on to something self-defeating? Often the beginning of healing means surrendering false securities to God with a prayer that God will step into the function they had in our lives. For example, we might pray that God heal a faltering relationship, that God direct and give courage for the demanding task, that God teach us who we are in our deepest selves. The decision to trust God in this way often opens the door wide to further healing.

We can clear the stream for God's work in us in additional ways. We can allow "bad" feelings to surface as we pray. Recognizing our anger, our lust, our doubts, and so on opens us to our brokenness, where God works. We can grow in willingness to surrender plans, habits of behavior and thought, or an insistence that things happen in a certain way. We can be willing to do the scary or difficult, such as ask someone for forgiveness. We can notice our rigidities and ask God that they be softened. If we catch ourselves saying things such as "I will never forget what he did to me," we can be willing to give up such ideas about how things have to be. We can become more supple, submitting all that we are to the loving touch of the Holy Spirit.

Although the healing process integrally involves our emotions, sometimes our emotions lag behind and our will must lead the way. For example, if we have been deeply hurt, we may not be able to change our feelings of anger, shame, or fear toward the one who hurt us. However, we can fully acknowledge these feelings, express them somehow, and then with our will ask Jesus to change our heart. God seems to honor this request with an outpouring of healing grace. Remember that Lois couldn't change her anger toward her father by herself, but by surrendering it to God she was deeply healed. Sometimes it seems that we have to go on sheer will for a time, but eventually God heals when we give all things over into God's hands.

As we continue to "clear our stream" of obstacles to wholeness, it is important to remember the wonderfully intricate interconnectedness of the physical, emotional, spiritual, and mental dimensions of the human person. We can trust God to bring to the surface whatever needs to be healed most in us, because we know that God wants "to grow" us. And we can trust that as we work with one area of our lives, God cares for the rest.

Issues in Physical Healing

Most people who are beginning to pray for healing focus on physical healing first. Physical healing has long been the province of TV healers, and, for some, physical healing is the only "real" healing. Even those of us who have a holistic view sometimes feel tempted to emphasize physical healing over healing in other areas of the person. Yet our particular experience is that the physical dimension is often the last to be touched by deep healing. And sometimes physical healing does not occur at all.

On the other hand, there have been many astonishing physical healings. Once Tilda prayed for a woman who had severe bursitis and was in great pain. Surgery was scheduled for the following week. The pain and the swelling vanished as they prayed together, and the woman has had no trouble since. As a matter of course, when Tilda leads a workshop to introduce the healing ministry, she often asks whether anyone in the room has a minor physical ailment, such as a headache or a cold. When the group prays for these small physical problems, the person is almost always healed or greatly improved immediately. This experience helps build the faith of a group of people in the effectiveness of healing prayer.

It is not clear why small physical ailments seem more readily healed than larger ones. After all, God has no more difficulty healing cancer than the flu. Nor is it easy to answer why someone might experience deep healing in her emotions and spirituality, and yet improve only a little in her physical problems. Experience shows that it seldom works the other way around: that someone is healed physically and not touched in emotions or spirit. Perhaps the faith of those who pray is a factor here. All of this says to us that God, working through our limitations and gifts, heals. If we are in physical distress, by all means we must pray with trust for physical healing.

As we pray, it may be important to pray with persistence. Sometimes it seems that physical healing happens only after praying for a period of time, say an hour or two, or weekly over many months. Francis McNutt calls this "soaking prayer,"[12] a process in which we direct our attention to a need for healing, and then rest in God's presence, inviting God to work through us. When we pray in this way, God seems to irradiate the person prayed for with love.

One woman prayed for with soaking prayer was losing the function of her kidneys. She was told she had at most two years to live. She was prayed for in a group once a month for sixteen months for about ten to fifteen minutes at a time. The prayer sessions were taped, and she listened to the tape daily at home. Three years later, she had more kidney function each time she was tested. Her doctors were mystified.

Issues in Emotional Healing

All of us have had experiences that hurt us and stunted our emotional or spiritual growth. For example, some of us have parents who belittled us or even physically abused us. Others have experienced tragedy or violence. Still others have been the victims of societal prejudice and hatred. Because of these experiences, some of us carry deep scars of sorrow, an abiding mistrust of the world, or emotional numbness. Probably each one of us can identify a need for healing in our emotions.

Faith Imagination

One of the most effective ways to pray for emotional healing is through a process called "faith imagination."[13] In this process, we use our capacity for imaginative thought as we invite Jesus to join us in the place where we hurt. This may mean going back in time with Jesus to a painful memory and reliving it with Jesus present. Or it might mean simply imagining Jesus in the room with us as we pray. Tilda, in her work with individuals, often witnesses Jesus responding to this invitation by working through the imagination to love someone back to wholeness. Sometimes, when a painful childhood scene is being relived, Jesus holds and comforts an adult who, for that moment, is a frightened child. Or he may act to protect her from those who hurt her, putting himself between a "child" and an adult abuser and receiving the abuse into his own body. This usually brings deep healing for the sufferer. Sometimes Jesus weeps, and, in other instances, he may involve a "child" in hilarious play. Often he speaks words that transform; sometimes just his presence makes all the difference. It is very moving to experience the myriad ways Jesus enters into the lives of hurting people through their imagination to bring exactly the kind of experience that will be healing for them. People who were the hopeless cases of psychotherapy have been marvelously healed. Jesus does indeed enter into our deepest pain, and there he "loves, transforms, forgives, redeems, resurrects, heals."

It is important to note that people vary greatly in the form their imagination takes. Some are oriented toward the visual and tend to imagine in pictures. Others never see pictures but imagine with hearing or bodily sensations. Accept the way *you* imagine, and allow God to communicate with you in whatever way God may choose.

As we try "faith imagination," we may be prompted to ask, "Am I making all this up?" People naturally wonder whether this kind of prayer means simply dreaming a rosy picture made of fantasy and wishes, with a little religion thrown in. It is natural to wonder whether this is prayer at all, or only an attempt to manipulate God instead.

To answer: It is possible to distort almost any process, including faith imagination. Even at best, our experience and expectations color all our perceptions. But God wills to get around our limitations.

Furthermore, it is striking how often the quality of the response from Jesus is not in the emotional repertoire of the one praying. For example, a deeply depressed individual cannot usually dredge up a heart-felt message of hope, no matter how great the effort. One who is terrified cannot find a way to feel safe just by thinking about it. Often a quality of "otherness" and surprise touches us through the action of God when we pray in this way.

However, the most compelling evidence that God is indeed at work in faith imagination is that people are healed. Pain that has been present for years may vanish or greatly diminish, and the healing seems to take deep root in the person. For example, Tilda was working with a woman who had been sexually abused by her father many times. The woman's picture of herself as a child was "a dirty kid, ashamed of myself, in a dirty dress with yucky stuff all over me." In her prayer, the woman saw Jesus come to the room she had when she was a child. He lifted her off the bed and took her outside to a river. There he washed her, gently and re-spectfully. Then Jesus gave her a new, pretty dress and helped her put it on. Later on, she reflected that the washing in the river was very similar to baptism, raising her to new life. But right then, she just felt marvelously clean. The prayer image ended with Jesus taking her to buy an ice cream cone. A year later, she continued to feel deeply cleansed by this experience.

Issues in Spiritual Healing

If we believe that God is healing us in any way, then we can be confident that God is touching our spirit, as well. To believe that God is at work in us is a joyful, marvelous thing. Conversely, physical or emotional pain has a spiritual component. Because of this, the more we welcome God's activity into every level of our being, the more we will be spiritually whole.

Spiritual healing is often simply a matter of being given in-creased trust, trust in God and in others. We may be enabled to give up our anxiety or worry in order to trust that God is at work. We may be given the grace to love and forgive someone whom we see as unlovable. As we feel God's love pouring over us, we may come to love ourselves more deeply, despite our brokenness.

One familiar form of spiritual healing is God's forgiveness of sin. We proclaim God's mercy each Sunday during community worship in the belief that God puts the past behind us and sets us on the path of new life. At the center of our faith is the belief that whenever we ask for forgiveness and are truly sorry, God always answers such a prayer with a yes. Consequently, genuine guilt can be addressed very easily by Christians. We simply ask for forgiveness and know that we have it. If we willingly accept God's forgiveness of all the sin of our life, we know profound healing. For many, such confession and forgiveness opens the door into the Christian life.

However, many can accept the *idea* of God's forgiveness but cannot allow this forgiveness to penetrate their hearts. In other words they cannot forgive *themselves*. A person in this state may need healing of his or her emotional woundedness or may need to "soak" in God's love over a period of time before God's forgiveness can cleanse.

Finally, recently ministers of healing have identified a type of spiritual healing called deliverance. The roots of deliverance prayer may be expressed in a statement: Jesus Christ, as victor over the forces of evil (Satan), endows Christians with the authority to address these forces in his name.

Jesus occasionally healed by commanding the forces of evil to depart[14] and commissioned his disciples to do the same as they preached the gospel.[15] Paul and his followers also ringingly affirmed Jesus' power over the forces of evil.[16] In deliverance prayer, we lay claim to the victory of Jesus over evil, commanding it to leave in his name.

This type prayer is called for only when *evil* seems to hold a person in bondage. This bondage apparently manifests itself to different degrees of severity. In addition, the evil forces seem to interact in a complex way with the sufferer's brokenness and particular personal history. A detailed discussion of deliverance prayer takes us far beyond the scope of this book. If you suspect a need for deliverance healing, read further on the subject[17] and use careful discernment. In addition, find someone wise and experienced to assist you before going ahead.

Certainly deliverance prayer should not be seen as magic, or an easy answer, or a way to simply get rid of what one doesn't like about himself or herself. In these matters we should avoid fascination with the power of evil and should keep hearts at rest in the power of Jesus Christ resurrected.

Although deliverance prayer is not ordinarily appropriate, it can be crucial to those who truly need it. In using it, we can bear witness to the marvelous power of Jesus to "bring deliverance to the captives"; we enlist the authority of Jesus over evil. For example, one woman was freed from frequent seizures after deliverance prayer; and another, from episodes of uncontrollable rage.

Being a Whole Person

It should be clear by now that whole persons are those on a healing journey. Praying for healing renews and deepens our relationship to God. Through it we discern God's will and surrender ourselves to God's work in us. This journey empowers us to be lovers and servants. As we are set free ourselves, we are also set free to give ourselves to others. This healing journey teaches us to find the gift in our suffering and brokenness. It leads us to expect that we will be transformed, and that what has been terrible in our lives will be redeemed, even turned into a gift. As one woman put it: "All my worst stuff has become my best stuff."

A final outcome of this journey toward wholeness is to be gifted with joy. Yes, God seems to want to heal us to empower us for effective ministry. But more important, God heals because God loves. In John's Gospel, Jesus describes himself beautifully as the vine and his followers as the branches. Then, perhaps gazing tenderly at his friends, he says, "These things I have spoken to you, that my joy may be in you, and that your joy may be full [John 15:1–11]."

As we continue on our own healing journeys, may this joy take root in us.

The Healing of a Tragedy

The story of Kathleen illustrates much of what we have been saying about the healing journey. Kathleen is a very active laywoman, the mother of three grown children and a person of prayer. This story concerns her son Jay.

Jay had been a little depressed and confused about what he wanted for a career, but no one thought he was deeply troubled. In his early twenties, he seemed to be a pretty normal young man. So it was a horrifying shock to Jay's family when he shot himself with a high-powered rifle. His disfigured body was discovered in his apartment.

Full of searing grief, Kathleen's spirit screamed "Why?" "Why didn't he come to us? We would have helped him. What did I do wrong? Why didn't I pick up the signals that something was so wrong? What drove him to this? Where was God? Why didn't God stop him?"

Her terrible pain began to express itself as tension in Kathleen's neck, jaw, and mouth. Over a period of two years she became more and more tense until her mouth was so tight that it drastically distorted her speech. Extensive medical tests found no explanation. Nothing organically wrong could be pinpointed.

When Tilda first met her, Kathleen's speech was almost impossible to understand. Her mouth seemed to be frozen into an expression of horror and pain. Sometimes she even looked as if she were gazing at Jay's mangled body.

She and Tilda worked together, mostly praying with faith imagination. As Kathleen prayed, she would usually sense Jesus standing in front of her. Sometimes he spoke, and his speaking addressed the questions of her heart. Sometimes his presence only comforted her. She often cried to him and felt he was somehow receiving her tears. Once she imagined Jesus cried with her, carrying her grief. Another time she felt the Lord inviting her to scream out her horror. She did this, even though she never remembered screaming before in her sedate family life. Very gradually her speech improved as she continued to allow the Lord to work in her.

At one point she discerned that she was subtly holding onto her speech impediment. She recognized it as a way of holding onto Jay. As long as she couldn't talk, his memory stayed alive. Soon, she was able to "give" Jay to Jesus to care for, and she visualized Jay walking arm in arm with Jesus. He looked happy and content. In fact, he was almost dancing. She found this image greatly comforting, and her speaking ability took a leap forward.

However, her healing still did not touch the deepest question of Kathleen's hurting heart. When Jay was alive, he had told her once that he believed in God but "not the same way you do, Ma." The memory of this conversation made Kathleen terribly afraid that Jay had not gone to heaven, because she assumed that he might not have believed in Jesus. Besides that, she wondered what God did about people who committed suicide. Would Jay be punished somehow? Would God really punish someone as upset as Jay must have been? She could hardly bear to think about this.

After trying to figure out an answer for months, Kathleen finally brought her questions to Jesus in a faith imagination prayer. In a marvelous outpouring of grace, she heard Jesus say to her, "Jay believed in God, so Jay also believed in me." She burst into tears, as months of tension and fear drained away. This answer was a powerful salve for her pain, and soon many other things began falling into place for her. Questions about the Trinity that had long troubled her, doubts about God's mercy and love, worry about Jay's soul—all seemed to be met in Jesus' simple answer. Kathleen looks back on this graced moment as one of the high points of her spiritual life.

Today Kathleen has a joyful, vibrant faith in God's love and an unshakeable conviction that Jesus stands with her through troubled times. She is more deeply compassionate toward others who are in pain than ever before. Although her speaking is much improved, she still has a slight speech impediment. The question of *why* still echoes faintly. She is still on the journey toward wholeness.

Chapter 4

A Simple Gift: Praying for Another's Healing

A Modern Story

Tilda tells the following story:

> A worried woman once brought her month-old daughter to a
> healing service to be prayed for. The baby's intestines were not fully
> developed at birth, so that her bowels could not move naturally. Her
> mother had been warned by her pediatrician that surgery would be
> needed if the baby's intestines did not mature quickly. In our process
> of discernment it seemed that God wanted us to pray for the physical
> healing of this child. We put our hands on the baby while the mother
> prayed an unrefined, heartfelt prayer: "O Lord, I love my baby!
> Please give us a poo-poo in this diaper." About a minute after
> beginning to pray, our prayer group heard the loveliest sound and
> smelled the most wonderful stink imaginable from the baby's bottom.
> The diaper was filled by the baby on her own for the first time, a
> concrete and beautiful sign that God was surely at work.
>
> The baby is now almost two years old. She never had surgery
> because from the time of the prayer on, her intestines worked just
> fine.

A Simple Gift

In the New Testament we read many such stories of people
bringing loved ones to Jesus for healing or asking Jesus to heal a

person from a distance. Recall, for instance, the paralytic lowered through the roof by four bold friends (Mark 2:1–12) or the epileptic boy brought to Jesus by his distraught father (Mark 9:14–29). Think of Jairus going to Jesus on behalf of his daughter (Mark 5:21–24, 35–42) or the centurion who approached Jesus because his servant was sick at home (Matthew 8:5–13). In the Gospels Jesus always responded to these requests by healing the person.

In this chapter we will explore more deeply what is involved in "bringing our loved ones to Jesus." We know healing prayer to be a simple gift, a profoundly moving way in which God shows love for us. God gives the gift of healing to the church, which invites, indeed calls, all of us to pray for the healing of others. [1]

Brother Roger, the prior of the Taizé ecumenical monastic community in France, once said that of all people, it should be small children who pray for healing. When healing takes place, there can be no mistaking that God is at work, not a powerful, influential leader. Ideally, when we as adults pray for healing, we become like small, trusting children—asking for what we want, telling our Parent where it hurts, and trusting the Parent to take care of it somehow.

Getting Out of the Way

While there is no technique for healing prayer, and certainly no system of prayer that can be applied to every situation, there are helpful suggestions about how to pray for healing and what seems best to avoid. People who pray for healing must let go of rules and techniques, so to make room for God to work. Much of the spiritual preparation for healing prayer has to do with knowing our helplessness and emptiness, on the one hand, and God's overflowing love and mercy, on the other. Prayer for healing means inviting God to work in the person in God's own way.

Certain temptations, however, threaten to place us in the way of God's action.

• We may be tempted to come to God as a grown-up who "knows best," who wants to be in control, who wants to appear competent, who has a good theory or theology, who perhaps even has special skills in a helping profession.

- Or our temptation may be to come to God armed with a rigid system of rules for healing prayer. Sometimes when prayers for healing are answered, we expect God to work in the same way the next time. Perhaps we have been led to pray in a particular manner, even two or three times. Then it is tempting to think that we have the healing process all figured out. We imagine we know how God will act in a particular instance. What began as a response to God's unique work with individuals becomes a pattern we try to impose on everybody. Of course, God won't be put into a little box—or a big one!

- We may be tempted to pray for the healing of others in a way that will make us look holy or satisfy our need to be powerful or needed. People tend to want healers on a pedestal, and it is very easy to oblige. Newcomers to healing prayer may not be tempted in this way, but most people who have had experience with healing prayer must face the temptation to self-aggrandizement sooner or later.

If we find we are eager for admiration and gratitude, if we begin to love how everyone calls us to ask for help, if we start to see ourselves as different and more holy than everybody else, it is time to confess the sin of arrogance and pride. We must pray for grace to see the truth: that we are ourselves wounded healers, simply channels God sometimes uses.[2]

One way to head off hero worship before it starts is to pray with a prayer partner or a team. Then when healing occurs, God, rather than the healer, more likely receives the credit. Further, in a team, members can helpfully watch for signs of pride in each other.

Of course we can certainly pray alone for someone and we should. But churches with healing ministries might consider adopting a healing team approach, so that no one is identified as the principal healer. A healing team also conveys the message that healing prayer is a ministry given to the church and not just to a few, unusually gifted people.[3]

- Another temptation persuades us to let the noise of our personal judgments and brokenness crowd out God's work. For example, once Tilda was asked to pray for a man who had strong urges toward voyeurism. That is, his desire was to peek through windows to watch women as they undressed. He had actually done this a few times and was making heroic efforts to control his compulsive behavior. He desperately wanted to be healed, and he felt terribly guilty for having these urges. He came for help, humbly hoping to be freed.

Tilda couldn't, however, see him as a struggling man whom God loved in his brokenness. All she was aware of was the loud judgment in her own mind: "How awful! Another man using women to get his kicks! How could he?" Obviously, Tilda was in no state to pray for this man, and not much happened during their time together.

It was only after he left that Tilda remembered how, as a child, she was very curious about how people's bodies looked and had done some peeking of her own when she was seven or eight. She realized that she had retained her own childish guilt, and that it had prevented her from loving this man.

Something very important needs to be learned from this story: If you are turned off, judgmental, scared, disgusted, shocked, and so forth, you probably have work to do with *yourself*. Something in you needs to be healed. In such a case, you would be well advised to let someone else pray for the other person until you work out your own issues. Remember, again, that we all are wounded healers.

• Another temptation leads us to put faith in our own skills or in our own faith.

In chapter 2 we examined the relation of faith to healing. When we put trust in the strength of our faith, or imagine that faith somehow manufactures healing, we simply betray our need for control. Although God surely does use whatever gifts we have, we dare not trust solely in our own intuition or learned skills. No matter how faith-filled we are, no matter what our skills and gifts, God heals. We put our trust in God, not in ourselves.

Often the professional person with many healing skills has the most trouble praying in simple trust, believing that God is already at work in the person who has sought prayers and in the healer, making up for what is lacking in faith or skills. A helpful approach is to seek counsel with a trusted friend, inviting him or her to tell you if you show any signs of putting faith in yourself rather than in God.

• The temptation arises to try to predict how God will work. It may momentarily give hope to say to the sufferer, "I know that

God will take away your cancer." But unless those praying for
another's healing are absolutely certain of this assumption through
discernment, their making such a statement reveals deep irrespon-
sibility. It would be much more faithful to say: "I don't know just
how God will answer us, but I do know that God loves you and
wants your wholeness. Let's invite God to use our prayers to do
whatever God wants."

• It is enormously tempting to pray for healing while insisting on
our agenda for the person prayed for. This does not mean that we
should pray only in vague generalities. It does mean that we trust
that God loves this person even more than we do and that God
knows better than we what is best. It is crucial to remember to pray
for specifics only after we have discerned what God wants to do for
the person.

The healing team of which Tilda was a part learned this in a
process that was both painful and deeply moving.

*Jeff, a young college student and a member of the track team,
found out that he had amyotrophic lateral sclerosis (A.L.S.), also
called Lou Gehrig's Disease. This terrible disease attacks the
muscles, including the heart and lungs, which simply disintegrate
and eventually stop functioning.*

*When Jeff first heard that he had about two years to live, he was
incredibly angry. He called it rotten luck. He swore. He yelled. He
cried. He couldn't stand to see anyone who was healthy or happy.
He was going to die, and he was certain no one cared, not even his
parents.*

*When our prayer team began to pray for Jeff, we prayed very
hard that he would be healed of A.L.S., that he would run again,
and go back to school. We prayed that he would not die. We prayed
with our own agenda.*

*We all liked Jeff a lot. It was very painful to see him each time
he came for prayer, because he had less and less control of his
muscles. His disease was progressing fast. The healing team was
bewildered and upset.*

*Yet God was powerfully at work. God met Jeff in all of his fear,
confusion, and despair, and started to change things for him.*

*Through our prayers Jeff felt prompted to deal with his parental
relationship. As he began to come to terms with his anger at his*

parents and with their rejection of him, he expressed his anger and let it flow away. Soon he forgave them and came to appreciate them for the first time in his life.

He also faced the fact that he had caused pain to a number of women friends. He would drop them after a few months of romantic interest after making promises to them that he had known he wouldn't keep. He started writing to the women, asking their forgiveness. Most of them wrote back, forgiving him and supporting him during his dying process. As these personal matters began to clear up in his life, Jeff began to feel better, despite the progressing disease.

Slowly people in the prayer group began to see that God was healing something within Jeff that we had never considered. It was hard for us to let go of our agenda for him, but the more we were able to surrender, the more Jeff seemed to benefit from our prayers.

As Jeff invited Jesus into his life more and more, his spiritual life deepened into radiance. He began to be so certain of God's love that he would say to people, "I know I'm dying, but I wouldn't exchange my life for anyone else's in the world. I know I'm dying, but I've been healed. I know I'm dying, but if I didn't have this illness, I would never have had this joy." And, indeed, it was obvious that Jeff was living in profound joy.

About a year before he died, Jeff began to be unafraid of dying. In fact he almost eagerly looked for it. Toward the end he experienced death as an adventure. He and a friend made a videotape of his last months. In it he tried to relate the message that even death for a Christian is finally not a tragedy.

Jeff touched very deeply all of us who knew him. None of us had hoped for this kind of healing in the beginning. We found it hard to give up our agenda and were terrribly saddened by his death. But clearly Jeff had been deeply healed, and it seemed that God had used our prayers.

In Jeff's story we catch a glimpse of the manner in which death provides the ultimate healing. Death sets us free from pain and all bondage.

This discussion of temptations and pitfalls might suggest that healing prayer is only for the saintly. Nothing could be further from the truth! Knowing that it is God who heals should give us the courage to pray for healing, even if we don't "have it together." Seeking discernment before we pray is a concrete way to put our faith in God, not in ourselves.

Before We Pray for Healing: The Discernment Process

The following presents an outline of a simple discernment process, such as we discussed in the previous chapter. Now we focus on praying for another.

• Invite God to use you as a channel of healing and to continue to give you whatever faith, discernment, and love is necessary to help the person you are praying for.

• Ask God to melt away anything in you that might get in the way—your need for power, your hang-ups or judgment, your brokenness, or your desire to cling to your own agenda. Know that God is able to use you *despite* these things.

• Feel your love and compassion for the person. Sometimes this is even more important than faith. Your own love for the person will probably carry with it your human desire for the person. Your instinct may be to say, for example, "I want this person to be healed, physically."

• Speak your desire to God as honestly and plainly as you can. Put your agenda in God's hands.

• Then, in silence, allow your agenda to be changed. Listen for the way in which God might want to heal this person. Ask God for what you should pray. Remember, even if a person is eventually healed physically, some other kind of healing may emerge first, for example, the release of anger.

• After inviting God to correct your agenda, trust that God will communicate with you in some way! Pay attention to pictures in your mind, hunches, intuitions, verses of scripture that come to mind, sensations in your own body, and the like. You might try to pray with faith imagination, seeing Jesus with the person. Remember, God speaks in many ways. It may be easier to trust what you discern when you're with one or more persons rather than alone.

• Once you sense God speaking in some way, ask yourself: "Does this seem consistent with the character of Jesus?" "Does it sound like the God of the Bible?" "Is it consistent with the best we know of theology and psychology?" "Does it echo the wisdom of the church?" For example, discernment that suggests someone is being punished for sins by God through illness and pain is very questionable, indeed. It is questionable because it does not meet the criteria of love and compassion.

• Proceed with your prayer, humbly using whatever discernment you were given. Act in faith, holding open the possibility that your discernment is incomplete or even inaccurate. Continue discerning each time you pray.

Say, for example, you discern an image of the person asking you for prayer. You "see" this person smiling and healthy, walking briskly through the woods. You might then pray: "Lord, please heal Jane. Restore her to health, that she may walk in joy with you."

Should your discernment consist of hearing the word *rest*, your prayer for healing might then be: "God, please help John to rest deeply. Let him completely rest in your presence, so that you renew every cell of his being. Help him to rest his anxieties and his pain in your everlasting arms."

Should you feel, as another example, sadness well up in you as you pray for discernment, you might share this with the one who has come for prayer. Ask whether he or she senses a pool of sadness within. Or you might simply pray: "Lord, if there is some deep sadness in Gary, we ask that you uncover it and enter into it with him. Heal him, so that he may claim the abundant joy you offer." Gary may not have said a word about being sad. He may have come expressing an entirely different need. But you would pray about sadness because you are acting in faith in response to discernment and because you know of the marvelous interconnection of body, mind, and spirit.

Also you would pray provisionally—"*If* there is some deep sadness . . ."—because you need always to keep in mind that you may not have accurate discernment. *Humble faith* is fundamental to healing prayer.

The story of Jim illustrates the important role of discernment in praying for another person. Jim came to a monthly healing service, suffering from ulcers. He had been in treatment for several years, but the pain worsened. As the healing team laid hands on Jim, he began to cry. One of the persons praying with him sensed these were tears of grief. Upon mentioning this, Jim told them that, although his mother had died several years before, he hadn't until this moment been able to shed one tear of grief. He marveled at how his tears were being released for the first time, as the healing team put their hands on his stomach pain. The team prayed that he continue to cry until all his accumulated grief was released.

By the next month, Jim's ulcers had improved. He had cried a lot, and he generally felt much better. As the team placed their hands on his stomach and asked God how to pray, Jim realized that he was still angry at his mother, who had become quite cranky and difficult to live with before she died. This important discernment came from the sufferer, rather than from the people who prayed. The prayer this time was that Jim be able to express his anger and then forgive his mother. Over the next month, he was able to do this, and his physical condition improved still more.

The third time Jim came for prayer, he realized that he felt guilty for neglecting his mother during her last months. The healing team declared God's love and forgiveness, praying that Jim be able to feel this forgiving grace in his body, especially in his abdomen. The following time the team saw Jim, his pain was nearly gone. He asked for prayers of thanksgiving for his healing.

Could the team have simply prayed for the healing of Jim's physical pain? Yes, of course they could have, and perhaps his ulcer would have been healed. But because discernment plays an important part in identifying the root cause of illness, it led to Jim's being deeply healed in emotions and spirit, as well as body.

When You Meet to Pray for Healing

We have been focusing on how to listen to God in a discernment process and how to prepare spiritually for healing prayer. We have just read accounts of how discernment can shape our prayers. Now we turn our attention to the actual process of praying with someone. Although prayers for healing can take place without the sufferer present, quite often you will want to pray face-to-face for someone in need.

Doing so has several advantages. First, careful listening to the person can help with discernment. Second, when you are physically present with people you can touch them in a variety of ways. You can put your hands on them or anoint them with oil. You can give them a hug or hold them as they cry. God uses our hands and bodies for healing, and touching often helps the one being prayed for to feel God's love. (More will be said about laying on of hands and anointing later in this chapter.)

Finally, when you are with someone, you can listen and respond to the story of their suffering. You can speak words of forgiveness. You can share your own faith. You can suggest soaking prayer or faith imagination. In other words, you can enter into a direct pastoring relationship with the one for whom you are praying.[4]

When you have the opportunity for this special caring presence, it is crucial to be as sensitive and respectful as possible. The following guidelines are for those who find themselves in such a pastoring role:

• Listen to the person who has sought healing. Let him or her know you are listening by putting the person's *feeling* in your own words. This can be part of the prayer itself or a brief comment you make before you pray. For example, a person may have had a cancer biopsy but does not yet have the results. Your response might be, "You sound so worried and scared." This sounds easy, but it takes lots of practice to do well. Friends can practice verbalizing feelings by listening to stories of each other's lives.[5]

• Listen to God. Pay attention to whatever discernment may come to you even as the person speaks.

• Don't give advice. You might be wrong. Even if you *were* right, you would have made the person dependent on *you.*

• Don't say, "I know just how you feel"—even if you have gone through a very similar experience. Remember that everyone's response is unique, and the person you are talking to may have reacted quite differently from you. Even if the difference is subtle, the difference must be respected.

• Witness to your own faith as you feel led, but from an "I" position. For example, to say, "Don't you know that God loves you?" may make a sick person feel guilty and wrong. And saying, "Remember that God loves you," can sound preachy. But if you say, "I believe that God loves you," you are simply bearing a witness to your own faith.

• Allow the person to cry. Let yourself relax in the presence of tears. Often gentle tears are the lubrication of God's action in a person. Provide tissues—and let the Lord work.

• As you pray with someone, be comfortable with periods of silence. You don't have to think up beautiful words. The words you do say can be very simple. Trust that the Holy Spirit prays through you "in sighs too deep for words [Rom. 8:26]" and will give you whatever words you need.

When it seems helpful to pray for a person using soaking prayer, we run out of words very quickly. Then we can just sit in God's presence with our hands on the person, trusting God to be at work. During soaking prayer you can visualize or otherwise imagine the person with Jesus. Watch what Jesus does; listen to what he says. Pay attention to what emotion he seems to show. You might want to ask the person for whom you are praying to invite Jesus into his or her imagination.

• Before you finish the prayer time, thank God for hearing you and for being at work in the person. In faith, ask God to continue the healing process.

Healing Rituals

Symbolic actions and the sacrament of Holy Communion, when used in the context of healing prayer, can be channels of God's grace and can send powerful messages to a person's inner being. The healing power of Jesus is released when prayers for healing are offered during the celebration of Holy Communion.

In addition to Holy Communion, some simple rituals are important to healing prayer. If those praying for another become comfortable with these rituals, the effectiveness of their ministry can be greatly enhanced.

• The most common ritual in healing prayer is the laying on of hands. Jesus modeled this ancient practice for us. He often healed by putting his hands on a person, and the early church followed his example. As when parents quite instinctively kiss or touch the place where a child hurts, touching is universally accepted as a way of saying "I love you." God uses this natural response of touching to heal and to bless others.

Of course, some people may be self-conscious about touching another person or of being touched. To help overcome this shyness try the laying on of hands a few times with a good friend. Many people find that it feels very natural and beautiful once they have had some experience with it. However, if you really cannot feel comfortable putting your hands on someone to pray for them, don't worry. Just pray, and trust God to work.

If you are able to touch during healing prayer, ask the person's permission before laying hands on him or her. You may want to put your hands where the problem is located. Therefore, if the person has heart trouble, you may want to touch his or her chest.

• A second ritual is confession and forgiveness. If someone confesses a sin, declare God's forgiveness. Any Christian can do this, for it is simply a matter of attesting to God's willingness to forgive. You might say, "Whenever we confess our sins and are sorry, God always forgives. In the name of Jesus Christ you are forgiven."

• A third ritual is anointing with oil. This action has roots in both the Old and New Testaments and has been practiced for centuries by some of the more liturgical churches. Anointing can be a deeply moving experience, like being filled with the balm of God's love. If the person agrees to be anointed, you put a little oil on your fingertip and rub it on the person's skin. You may put the oil either where the problem is (for example, on a broken leg) or you may trace a cross on the person's forehead. You might say: "(Name), I anoint you for healing in the name of Jesus. Let this oil soaking into your skin remind you of God's love soaking into your whole being—body, emotions, and spirit."

After the Amen

When the prayer is over, it is important to let go. The following are suggestions for doing so:

• Be absolutely trustworthy about keeping confidence. This means no one outside the prayer group should know anything about what was said during healing prayer time. Nothing can destroy a healing ministry faster than to be careless in this respect.

• As the person leaves, release him or her to God's care. Give up any burden you've taken on and any need to have the person be well according to your agenda. Ask God to heal any brokenness in you that has surfaced during the prayer. Then let God take care of you for a bit. Spend some time resting in God's presence, letting yourself be nourished.

• Continue to pray for the person regularly, but guard against carrying the person as a burden. Let Jesus do the carrying. Your part is simply to love and pray.

• Be sure to lighten up. As a healing ministry grows, it becomes increasingly vital to have regular time off for rest—for fun and silliness, for your own growth, for whatever renews you.

Putting it All Together

Perhaps all these suggestions and instructions sound a bit overwhelming. Actually, the practice of healing prayer feels very ordinary and simple. Much healing prayer takes place in informal ways in the normal context of friendship or family life. Often the prayers do not have to do with a crisis or with someone gravely ill, but just with the circumstances of day-to-day living. Healing prayer can flow naturally out of a minor event between two friends, as in the following story of Tilda's.

One day I had a date with my friend Julia. We planned to have lunch, then go to a large, empty parking lot near the beach. Julia had just received her New York State learner's permit, which gave her the right to practice driving. We had planned to have her first driving lesson in the parking lot with my car.

When I got to Julia's house, Julia answered the door, but she was limping. Her face was twisted in pain. She said her knee had begun to hurt and swell just that morning. She couldn't imagine what was going on, as she'd never before had any trouble with her knee. Julia thought we might have to postpone the driving lesson, because it was her right knee that was affected and she didn't think she could use it for the accelerator and brake.

We decided to see whether praying for a few minutes might help. As we prayed for discernment, I began to see Julia's face in my mind's eye. Her eyes looked scared. Then I "saw" her hunched in the driver's seat, holding the steering wheel with white-knuckled tension.

I asked Julia if she were scared. She replied that as we were praying she realized she was absolutely terrified of driving. She was afraid she would make some terrible mistake and that the car would "go crazy." She was afraid I would criticize and yell at her—as another teacher had. She knew rationally that these fears were not realistic, but they were there just the same. And it seemed that her fear was being expressed through pain in her knee. Both of us were well aware that the painful knee offered the perfect alibi for not having to drive that day. It "hurt too much."

We discerned that we needed to pray, not about the pain in her knee, but about her fear. I laid my hands on Julia's knee, and we prayed together that God would somehow address her fear of learning to drive. I said something like this: "God, you know how afraid Julia is right now, and you know how much her knee hurts. Please come into her fear and speak your truth into her heart. Heal her, Lord, of whatever is making her so afraid. Thank you for hearing us . . ."

Then we sat in silence, waiting. After a few minutes, Julia said that she was seeing a picture of herself in the driver's seat, but Jesus was sitting next to her. He was smiling, and she sensed that he was enjoying the ride. It seemed that he was telling her—although she didn't hear any words—that he wanted her to have the freedom of a driver's license.

As Julia told me how Jesus seemed to be responding to our prayers, she began to breathe sighs of relief, and her body relaxed. Her face lost its tension. She began to smile. A few minutes later the pain in her knee was almost gone. By the time we finished lunch, it was completely gone.

When we got to the parking lot for her lesson, Julia was still a little afraid. We needed to pause a few times to remember the powerful picture of Jesus sitting next to her and to thank him for his help. During subsequent lessons, her fear lessened. Today she has her own car and is a confident, safe driver.

Chapter 5

Praying for the Social Order

Over lunch in a Johannesburg restaurant, a white South African pastor spoke to Bob about his ministry. The pastor works mostly with blacks within as well as outside the church. Bob had seen firsthand how the pastor's daily life was an exhausting frenzy of activity, as he tried to meet endless needs for housing, jobs and health care, relief from government oppression, and so on. Also, the pastor lived in danger. His house had been raided by police, his office would be bombed. In his own white family he was something of an outcast. But, to his mind, his Christian activism was not extraordinary, but simply his response to the gospel in his situation.

The conversation turned to the pastor's inner religious life. Unconscious of the shift in tone, he described a simple, personal trust in God, a profound sense of being loved and led by Christ. God was real to him. When he spoke of the extensive pastoral counseling he did, it was in terms familiar to Bob: he prayed for healing as if his prayers would make a difference.

Asked if he experienced a tension between his activism and his piety, the pastor strongly rejected a distinction. Public ministry and private faith are absolutely inseparable, he insisted, and he couldn't conceive either apart from the other.

To those who struggle to hold together inner and outward expressions of faith, the pastor's testimony is very moving, because he lives his faith at such personal cost. Here is a man whose personal relationship to God is not a cop-out but the very source of his intense social ministry.

So far in this book our attention has been on individual persons, ourselves and others, as the subjects of healing prayer. Thinking of healing only with reference to individuals is not surprising. After all, at first glance it is the individual who is the focus of healing in the Bible and in traditional healing ministries. We may sense intuitively that the problems of social organizations, such as families, churches, corporations, and nations, don't lend themselves to the kinds of activities we have explored thus far. How can we lay hands on social ills or anoint institutions?

While this focus only upon individual healing may not be surprising, it is unfortunate. It limits our perception of the ways God works for social healing. We then may fail to lay claim to available spiritual resources in the struggle for justice and peace.

The South African pastor's story suggests another reason why the exclusive focus upon individual healing is unfortunate. It tends to perpetuate the alienating split between the private and the public expressions of religious faith, the inward and the outward journeys, between the activists and the pietists. We know in our hearts that dwelling upon only one of these is one-sided, a settling for a partial gospel. But we also know how easy it is to settle for a one-sided faith, given our differing religious visions, temperaments, and preferences.

The message of this chapter, however, is not just that activism and personal spirituality need to be held together. It is at once more limited and more novel. We want to *explore the distinctively spiritual resources of Christian faith for healing the brokenness of social institutions.*

Recognizing that it is vitally important for the church to be involved in social activism in all its forms, we ask: Is there something distinctive the church has to offer for the healing of social brokenness, something arising out of its unique vocation as the body of Christ? And if there is, how can the church go about imagining and instituting such social healing?

This is an area in which there are no experts. There are, however, provocative experiments and explorations that suggest much can be gained from raising these questions in the church.

Healing—The Social Dimension

We begin with the obvious: there is a need for social healing. Everywhere we look we see social brokenness and a deep need for God's grace to redeem the social structures in which individuals live their lives.

For example:

• A family system is so dysfunctional that it makes no sense to ask whose fault it is; the system itself is sick, and all its members are in some sense both victims and perpetrators.

• A congregation experiences internal conflict that seems to have a life of its own and lasts over many years as particular persons come and go.

• A sovereign nation behaves toward some of its citizens in ways that rob them of basic human rights, even of their lives. It is not that some individuals or classes are inherently evil, rather that they are trapped in interwoven systems of exploitation and suffering, which diminish them materially and spiritually.

The effects of social brokenness are evident on every side—in the pollution of air, earth, and water; in the poverty, homelessness, and despair of inner cities; in the national addiction to militarism and military spending. Upon reflection we come to see that the places where we live, work, worship, volunteer, consume, and vote are often connected to sick social systems.

Most Christians believe that social action is needed to address social brokenness. We willingly vote, lobby, organize, advocate, and act for the transformation of society. The question is, is spiritual intervention also relevant? Are social systems appropriate objects of healing prayer?

We believe the answer is yes. Recall the definition of healing in chapter 1. "Healing . . . is a process that involves the totality of our being: body, mind, emotion, spirit, *and our social context.*" While this could be taken to refer only to the healing of the individual *in* society, we here emphasize a more inclusive sense. Healing is a process that involves our social contexts, the healing *of* society.

The social dimension of healing is well stated in a paper of the Christian Medical Commission of the World Council of Churches. Health and wholeness, it says, is—

a dynamic state of well-being of the individual and the society; of physical, mental, spiritual, economic, political and social well-being; of being in harmony with each other, with the natural environment, and with God.[1]

Biblical Perspectives on Social Healing

The biblical God cares about and intervenes on behalf of the social order. This is evident in the very concept of peace, in Hebrew, *shalom*. In the Hebrew Bible Yahweh is portrayed as desiring the *shalom* of Israel as a nation. *Shalom* in biblical perspective is something other than inner tranquility. It is not simply peace and quiet. Rather, *shalom* describes a dynamic condition of social wholeness marked by justice, loyalty, and solidarity.[2]

After leading Israel out of Egypt, Yahweh caused bitter water to be sweetened and said to the people, "I am the Lord your healer" (Exodus 15:24–26).[3] Yahweh's healing consisted both of preserving the people's physical health and delivering them from Pharaoh's bondage. This is healing indeed. On other occasions in the wilderness period, Yahweh acted on behalf of the people as a whole, providing quails and manna to eat (Exodus 16), water to drink (Exodus 17), and various means of purification and atonement for the sins of the people (Leviticus 16; Numbers 19; 21).

The prophets speak of the redeeming work of Yahweh as a kind of healing. Malachi promises: "For you who fear my name the sun of righteousness shall arise, with healing in its wings [Mal. 4:2]." Second Isaiah speaks of the Servant of the Lord, upon whom was laid "the chastisement that *made us whole,* and with his stripes *we are healed* [Isa. 53:5, italics added]."

In the Gospels Jesus' healing of individual sufferers is a familiar theme. Healing social institutions seems not so explicit. Yet a closer look reveals a somewhat different picture. The central message of Jesus' preaching is the announcement of the coming "*basileia* of God." Sometimes translated "kingdom," *basileia* is both the realm (domain, or sphere of influence) where God holds sway and God's rule or reign over humanity (a relationship of sovereign authority). As such, the reign and realm of God is at least as much a social as an individual reality. Important as individual conversion was to Jesus, his main concern was the restoration of Israel as a people in the realm where God is sovereign.

Even Jesus' healings of individuals often evoke the social context of life and contain within them the promise of wider extensions of healing. His treatment of one person often had consequences for others. When Jesus stretched out his hand to heal a leper by means of touch (Mark 1:40–42), his gesture crossed an abyss of fear and religious taboo. It sent out the message that such a one was not to be cast out, as was the custom, but included in a new dispensation of compassion. When Jesus drove the demons from the man who lived among the tombs (and drove the five thousand swine into the sea!), his act would have had drastic economic consequences for all the inhabitants of Gerasa, whose livelihoods were threatened by the destruction of the herd. Reading between the lines we see Jesus shaking up settled socio-economic arrangements, casting out economic demons from the region along with the personal demons of the affected man (Mark 5:1–20).[4]

The event of Jesus' "casting out" the money changers from the temple is a kind of *social* exorcism (Mark 11:15–17).[5] Through this prophetic action Jesus "cleansed" the temple by exposing to the light of divine revelation what he believed to be the sin of the temple leadership. Social healing in this instance was a public demonstration of God's sovereign judgment upon a sacred institution gone astray.

Paul and his followers were keenly aware of the social dimensions of the conflict with evil. They warned of the threatening presence of "the principalities . . . the powers," the "world rulers," against whom the church had to arm itself spiritually as against worldly armies (see especially Ephesians 6:10–17; Colossians 1:15f., Galatians 4:3, 8f.).

In the Book of Revelation, the Roman Empire, symbolized as the whore Babylon, is the earthly embodiment of evil. The entire Book of Revelation can be read as an exorcism of the great dragon Satan and his minion, Babylon. At the end Christ triumphs over Babylon's oppression and idolatry. One can scarcely imagine a more powerful indictment of state evil than this. Through the medium of imaginative poetry, prophetic vision, and song, the truth about Roman rule is told in such a way as to renew and assure beleaguered Christian believers. Social evil, embodied in the state, was confronted, exposed, and dispatched by the prophet in a creative act of social healing.

These few examples from the scriptures of Israel and the church are relevant to social healing today. They show, sometimes between the lines but often explicitly that (1) *God wills the healing and transformation not only of individuals but also of the structures of society;* and (2) *the people of God employ various means of spiritual intervention to accomplish social healing.*

Two Case Studies in Social Healing

It is one thing to recognize that our understanding of healing should extend to the social realm and that God indeed wills the healing of churches and nations. It is something else to imagine how we can intervene spiritually for social healing. What is praying for social healing, and how does it differ from social action on the one hand and ordinary intercessory prayer on the other? Two actual cases may help us begin to imagine concrete acts of praying for institutional healing.

The Drowned Church

Description. A pastor was frustrated and baffled by the pervasive mood of hopelessness and negativity that had gripped her congregation for years. Nothing she tried seemed to help. "It won't work here," was the church's dominant mood. Also, the bitterness and strife among some members was evident as they lingered in the narthex before the worship service openly arguing and trading insults. Bible studies, prayer groups, and other activities that might build up the church held no interest. The pastor believed that the church as a whole was somehow sick, that there was an indefinable malaise blocking its growth and health.

Seeking support, the pastor asked a small group of clergy friends, people not associated with the congregation, to gather with her late one afternoon when there would be no one about the church. The plan was to pray for the healing of the church and discern the underlying sources of the church's malaise. The clergy would also celebrate Holy Communion for the healing of the congregation.

As the pastor's friends gathered, one noticed a commemorative plaque in a hallway. It stated that the church building had been erected at the expense of the local state government. This seemed quite unusual. The pastor explained that the original church building had been condemned by the state, which planned to build a dam and form a lake in the area. The state then paid for the relocation of the church building to its present site. At the time, the church members hadn't liked the move but had no say in the state's action. So everything of value had been removed, and the shell of the church building was covered by the waters of the newly formed lake. This had occurred almost a generation before. A few of the present members were children at the time of the move, but most had no direct memory of it. As the prayer group heard the story, one of them called it the story of the "drowned church."

The prayer group began by opening itself to the guidance of the Holy Spirit in order to discern how to shape their prayers and acts of intercession. What was the spiritual malaise the congregation suffered? As the group mediated about the church's experience, the image of the drowned church came forward again. It seemed the institution had suffered a trauma, just as an individual might. The church had a buried collective memory of losing something dear and holy. The grieving and sense of loss lived on in the institution, expressed in the undertone of defeat, negativism, and bitterness.

The prayer group was led to pray for the healing of the congregation's memory, specifically that the waters that had meant drowning and death to the church would be transformed into baptismal waters leading to new life. Later, as a symbolic ex-pression of this institutional baptismal renewal, members of the group moved through the church from room to room sprinkling water in each room in a gesture of blessing. Even as they did this, the oppressive atmosphere they had sensed earlier in the building seemed to lighten.

During Holy Communion, the group prayed for the healing of the congregation as a whole and for specific individuals who seemed to be foci of contention. They prayed for the pastor, that she be freed from any attitudes or behavior that helped perpetuate the church's illness. After prayer, as a sign and anticipation of the church's renewal, the group rang the church bell, loudly and joyfully.

The pastor later reported what happened after the group's spiritual intervention. The very next Sunday there was no one in the narthex wrangling. The people were in the pews, many of them praying! In the days immediately following the service, the pastor was astonished and delighted when several people, independent of each other, told her that they would like to see the church start a Bible study or other program. Although such a spurt of inquiry didn't last, it marked the point when things began to turn around.

Within a year, many new people had come into the church, and the lay leadership had almost completely changed. The church trustees had reversed themselves on forbidding Alcoholics Anonymous and other self-help groups from using the church facilities. One of the most significant changes was what the pastor called "a turn in the pastor's heart," so that she felt both more rooted and more protected. The pastor believes a connection existed between the striking changes in behavior and attitude of the congregation and the prayers and symbolic acts of the healing service.

Three years later, while the church still needed continued healing, in many ways it was a different church than it had been. A solid core of active lay people were committed to the church, and a weekly healing service prayed for the church's growth and well-being.

The prayers for the drowned church initiated a time of turning for the congregation. All the problems were not miraculously solved. But from that time on a shift of attitude, an opening to a new spirit and a new life, was made possible.

Reflection. What the pastor and her friends did was a form of prayer on behalf of the congregation. Of course, many people pray for institutions to which they belong. But this was different from what we usually think of as intercessory prayer. To begin with, the intervention arose out of the conviction that *prayer for the institution as institution* could make a difference. The group was prepared to think of the church as a kind of corporate person, with a history and a memory and a capacity for being hurt. They were led to this not by appeal to a sociological theory but from their belief that God loved that congregation for itself and desired that it be whole.

Second, the pastor gathered a *group* to pray with her. The members were not consultants and problem solvers, important as such people are, but people of prayer, discerners whose task was to be open to the inner spiritual dynamics of the congregation. As many people can attest, spiritual effectiveness increases in a group gathered for prayer. More important, perhaps, a greater capacity exists for spiritual discernment within a group than within an individual.

Third, *discernment* itself formed an essential part of the group's praying. In social healing discernment is a crucial beginning step for us in opening ourselves intentionally to the way the Holy Spirit wants to work in the situation.

Fourth, once the group's discernment had suggested a direction for their prayer, *ritual* played a key role in their work. In celebrating Holy Communion on behalf of the church, in sprinkling the church rooms with water reminiscent of baptism, even in pealing the church bell, the group expressed their prayerful intercession through intentional words and deeds. They acted in the prayerful hope that God would use their actions for the good of the church. Many people involved in praying for healing find, time and again, how rituals—both the historical rites and ceremonies of the church and acts designed especially for specific needs—are powerful means whereby God effects healing.

Fifth, the group *prayed for particular persons*, including the pastor. Institutional healing doesn't overlook the needs or the responsibilities of individuals who comprise the group, nor does it look for scapegoats.

Although these five observations are important, remember that the pastor's asking for these prayers did not provide an alternative to other means of addressing the church's problems. Enriched preaching and Christian education, conflict management, and other community healing interventions were important in that congregation. What this case does illustrate is the validity of a both/and approach to social healing, just as in personal healing. It is important to include intentional and imaginative acts of prayer among the many ways we seek to bring wholeness to institutions in which we live and work.

Finally, it surely will be in the minds of some readers that we really cannot say what happened in the case of the drowned church. We cannot objectively demonstrate a clearcut cause-and-effect relationship between the prayer group's intervention and subsequent changes. An elusive, inexplicable quality marks the events. For some this may be grounds for dismissing the whole thing as wishful thinking or coincidence. Increasing numbers of Christians, however, are not put off by their inability to explain the grace that seems to embrace us. After all, elusiveness and inexplicability almost always characterize God's working in human affairs! Rather, we sense the promise in such events and take the risk of praying in faith without needing to understand how our prayers work. Those who prayed for the drowned church entered into a ritual of social healing, sensing that this somehow released the healing power of God in the situation. That was enough for them to go on.

Social Exorcism

Description. The Reverend George McClain is a social activist in the United Methodist Church. Since 1974 he has been the Executive Secretary of the Methodist Federation for Social Action. A few years ago, in the course of his activities against South African apartheid, George was led to employ a form of spiritual action that was at once boldly innovative (as a means of social transformation) and entirely traditional (in its biblical roots). He has written a brief account of these activities from which we draw.[6]

George McClain developed what he calls "social exorcism" in the course of organizing a public demonstration against apartheid in front of the South African consulate in New York City in 1985. In addition to the usual prayers, speeches, and hymns, George led the assembled group in a declaration renouncing the spiritual power wielded by apartheid:

> We act today, in the name of Jesus Christ, to break the power of sin and death.
> We declare that in Jesus Christ the power of apartheid is broken and in the fullness of time will fall.
> We therefore renounce any power that apartheid in South Africa may have over our personal lives, over the United Methodist

Church, its agencies and conferences, over our investments or programs, or over our local churches and our ministries within them.

Uttered in the context of Christian ritual, the statement tacitly recognized that apartheid is an ideology with its own spiritual power. The statement dealt with this spiritual power in a manner appropriate to Christian faith, by declaring it ultimately subject to Christ and by renouncing any personal or institutional complicity with it.

To people accustomed to dealing with social and political issues as problems to be solved through the usual avenues of social action, such a ritual declaration may seem quaintly irrelevant. George McClain certainly felt the strangeness of it. Trained in the theological traditions of Tillich and Barth, he was led only slowly to social exorcism by a growing conviction that church people tended to have a limited vision of the church's unique role in social transformation. The church's ministry, he believes, "includes the exercise of spiritual as well as secular gifts for transformation."[7]

All too seldom have we prayed for institutional transformation . . . with an expectation that our prayers would be answered . . . and . . . paused quietly to discern either the root cause of the problem—the problem behind the problem—or what God wanted us—uniquely us—to do about it in that moment.[8]

A further impetus to George's work was a growing conviction about the nature of evil, that evil is not just the absence of good but, within individuals, can manifest an "independent, aggressive, God-defying quality." Further, he reasoned,

if evil has this quality, then it seemed that the power of Christ to cast out the emissaries of this evil was not just a sort of embarrassing and undigested aspect of the New Testament's witness, but a real necessity.

And in terms of my own social action ministry I began to ask the question, "Are not institutions, as well as persons, often held captive by evil powers; and if so, what is the ministry of the church toward them?"[9]

George's experiments with this approach to confronting social evil continued in a confrontation with a particular denominational agency charged with investing church pension funds. Against the wishes of the General Conference of the denomination, and most vocal opinion in the church, the agency refused to divest its stock holdings in companies doing business in South Africa or even to press the companies to stop doing business with the apartheid economy. Despite numerous attempts by anti-apartheid activists to influence the agency, including resolutions, petitions, meetings, picketing, and civil disobedience against the agency, the situation was at an impasse.

In a summer retreat setting during this time, George and a few associates expressed their deep frustration and sense of failure. Some members of the group were experienced with liturgies of deliverance for individuals, and one of them suggested that the group, then and there, hold a ritual of social exorcism modeled on a service of individual exorcism. In this way they would seek God's help in breaking the chains that linked the church and its agency with apartheid. The group prepared such a liturgy.

The service of social exorcism began with time for discerning what were the ungodly spirits blocking the church. The group concluded that they were the spirits of fear and intimidation, arrogance and lust for power, mammon, and patriarchy. A statement of purpose included these words:

> We gather . . . to proclaim Jesus Christ as the ultimate authority over all beings, structures, and institutions. All spirits, influences, or powers, recognized or unrecognized, which are not of God, are in principle defeated or self-defeating and have in Christ been exposed as fraudulent. We offer ourselves as instruments of God's power and sovereignty over the power of evil.[10]

There followed the reading of Colossians 1:16, which declares the authority of Christ over all the powers of the created order. They then confessed any way they personally were in complicity with the spirits they had identified. Following the sharing of bread and cup, they spoke solemn words severing any ties between the agency and past negative influences, and solemn words casting out the spirits whose negative influence had been discerned:

Spirit of fear and intimidation, in the name of Jesus Christ, we order you to depart from [the agency] and go to Jesus.[11]

The service continued with prayers of support and renewal for the individual members of the agency. The group concluded with prayers for each other in their roles in the anti-apartheid struggle.

Exhausted after the lengthy service, George and the others sensed the power of the ritual in which they participated, and they felt that something within themselves had changed.

The following weeks brought an unexpected, dramatic change in the situation. The key figure in the agency's long-held policy about divestment quite unexpectedly announced plans to resign. Suddenly there was an opportunity for a new policy under new leadership. Could that little group of seven activists claim a cause-and-effect relationship between their service of social exorcism, the resignation, and subsequent events? George McClain says, "This connection may not be deduced through ordinary cause-effect analysis, but in terms of the 'logic' of the Spirit and her movement among us, I believe there was a powerful relationship."[12]

That was not the last of the surprises. At a meeting three months later, decision makers in the agency itself showed a very perceptible change in their attitude toward the issue of divestment and toward the activists. That changed attitude continued through the following months, expressed in positive steps to bring the agency's policy in line with the wishes of the denomination as a whole. On their part, George and the other activists experienced a kind of conversion in their attitudes toward the members of the agency, seeing them not as adversaries but as men and women trying to carry out a difficult trust to the best of their abilities. George and others continued to act in the belief that the struggle was not simply a matter of policy advocacy but of an engagement with spiritual powers.

It is important to note that the activists were not identifying particular members as evil persons. George wrote of the members of the agency:

Actually we believe them to be dedicated, responsible, even exemplary, Christian people. Rather we address this board collectively as trustees of an institution which is blocked from doing God's will in relation to South African investments. In this regard the board is held captive by alien influences and stands in need of a healing ministry which we here seek to perform. [13]

George McClain's own reflections on social exorcism provide a fitting conclusion to this story. "This whole experience suggests to me very strongly that we need to employ our spiritual gifts as part of our witness to God's transforming love and power." He concludes:

Walter Brueggemann suggests that in our era God is at work dismantling the Enlightenment worldview, with its unduly rationalistic, controlling and dominating characteristics. I find this assertion quite illuminating, for it witnesses to a living God who is inviting us to a more complete view of the universe as physical *and* spiritual. The shattering of our overly rationalistic worldview is part of that invitation. Only then can be begin to place the full range of our spiritual life and gifts at God's disposal in the struggle for the social transformation which God is stirring up. [14]

Reflection. This case has several things in common with that of the drowned church. (1) A group acted in the belief that their prayers could make a difference. (2) It was crucial that the group gather as the body of Christ. They benefited from shared insights and provided a check against individual pride. (3) Their first act was to try to discern the true spiritual situation, the problem behind the problem. (4) In response, they drew upon and modified traditional rituals of the church (in this case, Holy Communion and exorcism). (5) They acted on behalf of individuals as well as the institution as a whole and did not overlook their own need for forgiveness and healing.

The case has unique aspects, as well, arising mostly out of the participants' willingness to think about social evil in a certain way. They acted in the belief that evil has an "aggressive, God-defying" character. When they saw apartheid as not only a set of political and economic arrangements but also as a veritable legion of evil spirits arrayed against God and working ill against all who are touched by it, then the possibility was opened for a deeper and more telling assault than that offered by political measures alone.[15] Seeing evil in this way, the group acted on the basis of the New Testament faith in Christ's victory over Satan. In essence their services of social exorcism were declarations of the way things are under God.

Social exorcism is truly an act of faith in the ultimate triumph of righteousness. Its authority resides in its connection to divine truth, which, once told, may begin to transform the present moment.

The power of social exorcism resides in the victory of Christ over sin and death. Christians confess that no structure of society, no "principality or power," lies outside the sphere of God's creative and redemptive care. Hard as this may be to believe in regard to individual brokenness, it is even harder to affirm in the face of the massive human suffering brought on by social evil. How are we to reconcile this faith with the testimony of our senses, which, for example, sees apartheid flourishing after its demons have been exorcised in the name of Christ? What, after all, has been transacted in a ritual of social exorcism?

At the very least, social exorcism is *an act of revelation,* in which evil is unmasked and the truth is told. Walter Wink writes:

> The march across the Selma bridge by black civil rights advo-
> cates was an act of exorcism. It exposed the demon of racism,
> stripping away the screen of legality and custom for the entire
> world to see. . . . The act is efficacious simply by virtue of its
> bearing witness to the truth in a climate of lies. . . . But the
> point of collective exorcism is not in the first place reform, but
> revelation: the unveiling of unsuspected evil in high places.[16]

Beyond that, social exorcism is *an act whereby evil is addressed and dealt with on a spiritual level.* The spiritual intervention made a difference. The attitude of a church agency changed subtly but significantly, and new possibilities were opened. This is not to be understood in rational cause-and-effect ways but in what George McClain calls "the logic of the Spirit." God used the prayers of the community to work creatively for healing.

However, it may not be possible to say what is transacted in social exorcism or to agree in explaining it. It is fair to say that the group could not explain rationally what it was in which they were engaged. They acted out of obedience to a biblical way of confronting evil, trusting that God would use their efforts. But as with virtually all our experience of the grace of God, we participate in it and receive its benefits before we understand what we have experienced.

A Group Exercise in Social Exorcism*

A group wishing to explore social exorcism may undertake the following process. It should be entered into soberly, prayerfully, and expectantly.

Begin by asking each person in the group to consider what social institution or social issue exerts the most dehumanizing influence upon him or her personally. The question to ask is this: What makes me feel heavy and weighed down? After time for reflection, share your feelings and agree to focus the group's attention upon one institution. Any institution may be named—family or church, school or business, a multinational corporation, an agency or branch of government, an ideology or social pattern that has institutional expression. Together, enter into the following process:

1. *Discern the powers' identity.* Ask yourself: What are the spiritual forces at work in this institution? In silence, be open to any images, ideas, words, feelings that come. Name them, together. For example, you may identify a spirit of greed, or of domination, and so forth.

2. *Confront the powers within.* Ask yourself: What stands in the way of my being free of these powers? How am I in collusion with them? How am I hooked by them? Examine motives, ambitions, addictions. For example, if you have named a spirit of greed, then you need to confess how you allow greed into your life.

3. *Put on the whole armor of God.* Read aloud Ephesians 6:10–20. Equip each person with the spiritual armor named in the passage. Ask what specific armor is especially needed by those most

---

*This exercise was devised by George McClain and is used with his permission.

affected by these powers. For example, for one oppressed by a spirit of cynicism, arm her or him with the "shield of faith." Other members of the group can then lay hands on the person to signify this arming.

4. *Pray expectantly to contain evil.* Seek protection from the aggressive assault of the powers by invoking the protection of Christ.

5. *Lay tangible, persistent claim of God in Christ upon the institution.* Do this verbally, in bold words of command, invoking Christ's victory over the demonic powers. Say, for example, "Spirit of cynicism, in the name of Jesus we order you to depart from this institution and go to Jesus."

At the end of the exercise, take time to give thanks, in faith releasing your service to God.

A Final Word

There is much to learn about praying for social healing, and it is important for churches to explore such prayer. The two cases examined above may lead you to see situations in your own experience that you can address by some form of social healing prayer. Most important, you may be moved to continue the exploration in your own ways, according to your sense of the call of God and the needs of the social order. You may find "Praying for an Institution" in the Appendix of this book to be of help.

Chapter 6

The Church as a Healing Community

When we speak of the church as a healing community, we think very concretely of local congregations and religious fellowships. But we think of them also as healing communities in three interconnected senses.

Healing communities are *communities of people who know they need healing.* People broken in spirit, body, mind, or relationships come to them to find support and healing. Second, healing communities are *communities of healers.* People in such communities, despite their own woundedness, stretch out their hands to persons and institutions in obedience to Christ. Third, healing communities are *communities in process of being healed.* In them reconciliation and liberation, justice and peace are emerging as qualities of community life.

In this chapter we evoke a sense of what it means for churches to become healing communities, and to do this we draw upon two remarkable biblical portraits. Then we look practically at how to start a healing ministry in a local church.

Summoning the Elders

In James we find a passage not very well known in mainline Protestant churches. Read it from the perspective of the holistic healing we have been examining:

Is any one among you suffering? Let him pray. Is any cheerful? Let him sing praise. Is any among you sick? Let her call for the elders of the church, and let them pray over her, anointing with oil in the name of the Lord; and the prayer of faith will save the sufferer, and the Lord will raise her up; and if she has committed sins, she will be forgiven. Therefore confess your sins to one another, and pray for one another, that you may be healed. The prayer of the righteous has great power in its effects. [1]

A Presbyterian minister tells about an event that took place years ago in a church he served in northwestern Pennsylvania. Tom, a faithful, long-time member of the church, for some time had suffered from cranial cancer. He had lost sight in one eye and full use of a leg and an arm. A team of surgeons trained at the Mayo Clinic had opened his skull and done for him as much as they could. The disease was bound to run its course and result in Tom's death.

While Tom was in the hospital, he called the pastor to say that he was giving up on medical care. Moreover, he said he had read a passage in James where he discovered that "the prayer of faith shall raise the sick . . . and if he has committed sins, he will be forgiven." Tom then did something quite unusual in his church. He asked the pastor to convene elders and to come with them to the hospital in order to anoint him with oil and pray on his behalf.

All this was new for the pastor, and he was not completely sure how to respond. But sensing that the ritual could be reassuring to Tom, he went to the drugstore, bought some oil, and gathered the elders.

The elders, not used to playing this role, also were surprised by Tom's request. Yet they readily agreed to come and pray, glad for a way of expressing their concern for their friend and perhaps sensing that in this way God could use them for Tom's benefit.

So the pastor and elders gathered around Tom's hospital bed. They read the passage from James, laid hands on Tom, and said prayers. The pastor touched Tom's forehead with oil in the name of Jesus. Tom made a confession of sin and heard the group pronounce God's forgiving love. When they finished, nothing dramatic happened—to no one's surprise—but Tom seemed to be at peace.

After the anointing service, Tom did not regain the use of his eye or his limbs, but from that time on the progress of his cancer was arrested. More than two decades later, no further evidence of the cancer could be found. To the amazement of his doctors, his pastor, and the whole congregation, Tom has lived to tell anyone who will listen about his service of anointing! Tom's remarkable story highlights the importance of the local church as *the* locus of Christian healing.

For his part, Tom displayed an innate wisdom in sensing what he needed from the church. And the church—in the person of the pastor and elders—somehow had the grace to let itself be used by God. Whatever mixture of sympathy, awkwardness, and obedience the pastor and elders brought to the moment, God used it all for Tom's good. What happened to Tom reminds us that *the church is most truly the church when it puts itself at God's disposal and lets the Holy Spirit use it to heal and transform.*

The story of Tom's healing and the passage from James provide a number of leads into thinking of the church as a healing community. First, Tom was a loyal churchman who somehow knew where he needed to be in his hour of need, namely, surrounded by the church—literally! He might have hauled himself to a large and impersonal healing service led by someone with a "gift of healing." Many people do, and some are helped. The appeal of the James passage was that it directed Tom to the community where he had always sought God's grace and where, he decided, he would seek it again. *Every Christian congregation has the potential for being a community where healing takes place.*

In thinking of those Presbyterian elders, we should appreciate the ordinariness of the people who had a role in Tom's extraordinary healing. We may assume they exercised spiritual trusteeship in the congregation as elders are supposed to do, but surely in their own eyes they possessed no special powers, no healing gifts. They did not need to, and that is the point.

The Letter of James reflects its roots in ancient Judaism, which had great confidence in the power of a holy person's prayer. But we should not suppose that only "righteous" elders are worthy to do what Tom's friends did or that people need some great measure of faith to be used in healing. The elders' obedience, not their righteousness—or, should we say, their righteousness *as* obedience—should be what impresses us. Such obedience no doubt mixed their wish to support their friend with their sense of responsibility to their elder's office and perhaps with a hope against hope that God would somehow use their efforts. They lived out what we might call an "ordinary obedience," the kind each of us may imagine ourselves living out in our churches, one without pretense or heroics. *Christian churches are called to become communities of ordinary obedience to the Spirit's healing activity in their midst.*

The story of Tom's healing demonstrates another, subtler shade of obedience. Tom surprised his pastor by appealing to the little-known religious rite we have already discussed—anointing—described in James 5. Tom's request for anointing probably also surprised the elders. But in the end they all gave themselves to the act of anointing, out of some sense of faithfulness to the plain sense of the scriptural word.

We who pride ourselves on being modern and "with it" may find what the elders did almost embarrassingly naive. But those with experience in healing ministries can testify that the Spirit addresses us through the plain sense of the Bible when we open ourselves to it. This is especially so when we imaginatively and expectantly enter the Gospel healing stories. We affirm solid biblical study and vigorous biblical criticism, which are essential for the interpretation of scripture in the church. But *when in simplicity as the church we give ourselves to the enactment of the biblical words, we trust that the Spirit will use us and work through us for healing.*

Finally, notice the strong connection in James 5 between healing and forgiveness of sin. We have already seen in chapter 3 that an inability to forgive or accept forgiveness can erect a barrier to physical and emotional healing, and that confession and forgiveness can lead to deep spiritual healing.

In James 5 the emphasis rests on a community setting in which sin is confessed and forgiveness pronounced. In many churches confession and forgiveness occur regularly in worship through spoken acts. Pastoral counseling and spiritual direction also provide opportunities to confess sin and receive forgiveness in more intimate settings. In these settings the whole church is represented in the pastoral and priestly office. The Christian community, therefore, can always create a climate where, individually or in small groups, persons feel free to acknowledge their sin and where they seek forgiveness and reconciliation.

The author of James was wise in the ways of the human soul. He knew the difference between curing the illness that afflicts a person and healing the person—body, mind, and soul. In the latter, the sufferer's relation to God and neighbor is an indispensible factor. Healing that is Christian always reaches into the moral and spiritual dimensions of life. *It is the unique vocation of the Christian community to minister to the whole person.*

Entering a Partnership of Giving and Receiving

Christian healing also encompasses the practical affairs of life, matters of health, welfare, and daily sustenance. One of the most vivid New Testament portrayals of a healing church might not even be identified as such at first glance. Nothing is said of great miracles of healing being performed among the Philippian Christians. But their service to their beloved apostle Paul proved nothing less than a ministry of holistic healing. He writes them:

And you Philippians yourselves know that in the beginning of the gospel, when I left Macedonia, no church *entered into partnership with me in giving and receiving* except you only; for even in Thessalonica you sent me help once and again. . . . I am filled, having received from Epaphroditus the gifts you sent, a fragrant offering, a sacrifice acceptable and pleasing to God.[2]

What did the Philippian church do for Paul? More than once they sent gifts of money to support him in his missionary work. Paul boasted to the Corinthians that he had not accepted help from them (1 Corinthians 9:3–15; 2 Corinthians 11:7–9). But with the Philippians he entered into a "partnership of receiving."

This partnership also included moral support during some of Paul's harshest days. Even as he wrote, he didn't know whether he would survive his imprisonment: "You are all partakers with me of grace, both in my imprisonment and in the defense and confirmation of the gospel [Phil. 1:7]."

The church expressed partnership in the most direct sense by sending one of its members to minister to Paul on their behalf. This Epaphroditus Paul calls "your messenger and minister to my need," and "my brother and fellow worker and fellow soldier [Phil. 2:25]." He nearly died while with Paul, "risking his life to complete your service to me [Phil. 2:30]." Others from Philippi, including the women activists Euodia and Syntyche, also labored alongside Paul on behalf of the church (Philippians 4:2).

Undergirding and no doubt motivating all the practical support Paul received from the Philippians were their constant prayers on his behalf. He will continue to rejoice, he says, "for I know that through your prayers and the help of the Spirit of Jesus Christ this [imprisonment] will turn out for my deliverance [Phil. 1:19]."

The church in Philippi stretched out its hands to sustain and support its friend in the specific ways he most urgently needed. In so doing, they also became recipients of grace. They had already received much from Paul: their very existence as believers. He promised more. "My God will supply every need of yours according to God's riches in glory in Christ Jesus [Phil. 4:19]." Truly, the Philippians experienced being a healing community, in a partnership of giving and receiving.

A struggling, inner-city United Methodist church entered into a partnership of giving and receiving with a woman named Maria. This story at first seems utterly removed from Paul and the Philippians. Beneath the surface, however, weaves a common theme.

Because of hospital overcrowding, the intensive care unit of a state mental hospital released Maria onto the streets. She had known a lifetime of neglect and cruel abuse and at the time of her release was seriously impaired socially and emotionally. Soon she came to the attention of some people in the United Methodist church in her neighborhood. By then she was a young single mother with an infant, living on welfare and completely unequipped to take care of herself and her child. The one anchor Maria had was a skillful therapist willing to work with her without pay.

But Maria needed help in managing the daily affairs of her life to sustain her through years of therapy and adjustment. Some church members stretched out their hands to Maria and her child with countless deeds of practical love. They gave her rides to the doctor and to the welfare office, provided baby-sitting, rustled up clothing for the child. They helped find secondhand furniture for her apartment and patiently taught her the basics of money management. Through it all they extended companionship, becoming friends whom she could talk to, who lent a sympathetic ear. Maria was an emotionally needy person, too draining for one or two people to deal with alone for very long. But the church community could distribute Maria's needs among them and in that way hang in with her.

Six years after her release from the hospital, Maria was still on a healing journey. But all the church's time and love and companionship—plus her therapist's help—had made a big difference. She was taking courses at a local college and seeking a part-time job. Her child was well-adjusted and doing very well in school. She was a confident adult with a rapidly growing sense of self-worth and a feeling of hope about the future.

That's not the end of the story, however. Naturally gregarious, Maria had befriended the woman minister of a nearby storefront church. When the little church lost its lease, the minister didn't know what to do. So Maria brought her to her own United Methodist friends with the suggestion that they lease space to the storefront church. The United Methodist congregation could use the added income, so an agreement was reached. It delighted all parties. Maria proved to be an angel to both congregations! Later, she produced beautiful drawings for the church's anniversary celebration. Though no one could have predicted Maria's future when the church people began to reach out to her, the church and she entered into a partnership of giving and receiving.

Whether in acts of prayer or deeds of service, a healing church asks how the Spirit wants to work in the lives it touches, and then the church tries to make itself available for that work. *A healing church sees that doing God's work in human lives always leads to healing,* whether expressed in healing of bodies and minds, giving money, supporting one in need with countless practical deeds of love, or giving people time and space to grow. Not least, a healing church knows itself as the recipient of gifts from a God who, as Paul says, will supply its every need out of the richness of Jesus Christ.

How to Start a Healing Ministry in Your Local Church

At this point let us shift gears from seeking to spark imaginations to giving suggestions for realistic planning.

Suppose you have caught a vision of your local church as a healing community. Though the idea scares you a bit, you see it as a natural and exciting response to Jesus' invitation to stretch out your hand. You sense the spiritual renewal that could touch your church if it began to trust God in this way. Most of all, you see the need for healing all around you, as well as in your own life, and you believe God wants to use your church to help make people whole.

Now the question becomes, how do I go about translating dreams into reality? What are the beginning steps? Following are practical how-to's, which draw on the experiences of many churches that have started their own healing ministries.

Start with yourself, with praying and listening. We have talked a lot about discernment in this book. In beginning a church healing ministry, discernment again is crucial. Listen to the Spirit. Ask yourself: Is this a ministry the Spirit is nudging my church toward? What specific needs do I see? Am I being called to take the initiative? Does the idea scare me? Excite me?

Live with the idea over time to see where—and to whom!—the Spirit leads.

Also, examine your motives for being attracted to healing. Ask yourself: Am I really looking for healing for myself, or do I think it's only "they" who need healing? Am I drawn to the idea because it's a fad or because it's safer than social action? What needs to happen within me in order for me to be able to pray wholeheartedly for others?

An invaluable resource for this process of listening to the Spirit is Bible study. Go especially to the healing stories of the Gospels, leisurely recreate the scenes, enter them personally by putting yourself in the presence of Jesus the healer.[3] Expect Jesus to surprise you, and be alert to images, words, and feelings that arise.

Gather a group of like-minded persons. From the beginning be on the lookout for people to share your concern. They may be close friends or people you hardly know. They may be the folks always in prayer groups or people you wouldn't have guessed might be interested. Our experience is that almost every community has in it people who have been healed or who feel gentle nudgings toward healing prayer but who, for whatever reason, have not shared their feelings with others. Part of your job is simply to be watchful for those whom the Spirit puts in your path. Once people learn of your interest, you will probably not have a problem finding kindred spirits.

What do you do when you find people who respond? Gather as a group, whether two people or ten, to discern what should be happening in your church. Focus on listening to the Spirit through prayer, silence, Bible study, and discussion. Share your own needs for healing, and pray for each other. Don't hurry the process. As we have often said before, you will find your energy and sensitivity multiplied in a group.

Involve laity and clergy. If you are a layperson neither run *to* the pastor nor do an end run *around* the pastor. The ministry of healing should not be the responsibility of only the pastoral staff of a church. Healing prayer is a ministry of the whole church. It is important to emphasize this because laypersons sometimes just assume healing prayer is something specialized, or something for the professionally religious, so they may sit back and wait for the pastor to initiate action.

On the other hand, it would be a mistake to go very far in exploring healing prayer without involving the clergy. Generalizing about clergy attitudes toward the subject of healing is difficult to do. Often a layperson will say in a workshop, "Why isn't my minister interested in this!?" And it is true that for a variety of reasons many ministers *are* unacquainted with or apprehensive about healing in the church. But there are also clergy who bemoan their congregation's apathy toward healing services they try to initiate.

As a layperson, recognize the wide variety of styles of pastoral leadership and congregational organization, and bring the clergy into the exploration early on. Continue to be alert to the ways the Spirit wants to use *you*.

Ask together what style of ministry would suit your church. "Style of ministry" means habits of congregational life as they are shaped by denominational and confessional heritage, patterns of worship, social ethos, demographics, shared memories, and so on. The needs of a rural congregation of Mennonites may differ from those of an urban Roman Catholic parish. A small congregation whose average age is sixty will have a different style from a young and growing church of the same denomination. Also, pay attention to preferred styles of worship when developing your healing ministry. Sacramental, charismatic, and free churches, for example, will select types of public healing services noticeably different from each other.

Ask together what forms of healing prayer will best suit your church. Ideally, this is a decision in which the whole congregation should be involved, but it is good to start thinking about a form at this exploratory stage. An almost limitless variety of ways Christians can gather for healing exist. The distinctive needs, gifts, and personality of your church will suggest the right kind of prayer for you. Of course, you can expect this to change and evolve over time. Three ways of structuring a ministry of healing in a local church setting are (1) public worship, (2) healing prayer groups, and (3) healing teams. These will be described in more detail below.

Bring your desire for a healing ministry to the church leadership. So far you and your friends have been listening and imagining possibilities, not making decisions for other people. At some point you need to take your concern to the official structures of the church. Remember that it is extremely important that *a healing ministry be understood and supported by the whole church.* Too long relegated to the margins, healing needs to be brought into the center and given institutional sanction.

Two things should happen almost simultaneously in this process: consultation and study. Communicate your vision of your church as a healing community to those responsible for the worship, the spiritual life, and the social concerns in your church. Tell your own stories. Invite others to explore the possibilities for your church, beginning with their own need for healing. Remember that it is not first a matter of another new program but of a response to a call.

While personal testimony is vital, it is also vital for people to define terms, deal with questions and doubts, examine various styles, and, most important, experience for themselves God's healing presence and love. Invite church leaders and decision makers to gather for short courses that include Bible study, reading and discussion of good books on the subject of healing, and experiences of healing prayer.[4]

What institutional form your church's healing ministry takes will depend on many variables. Initiative may reside in the pastoral staff, in a standing committee, or in a newly formed structure. You personally may be at the center of it, or you may need to pass your vision to others. What is important is that the whole church hears Jesus' invitation and the whole church begins to "stretch out its hands" in ways that will take root and grow in the lives of the people.

Be a healer in your community. Despite our best efforts and hopes, sometimes things don't work out the way we want them to. Others don't share our vision of healing in the church, or the time isn't right, and so on. Whether or not your church develops a structured healing ministry, you can still respond to your call by being a channel of healing among your friends, your family, and the community.

Expect the Holy Spirit to show you the way. The last word in our discussion of practical steps is an encouraging one! If we believe that God is calling churches to a renewal of healing in our time, then we can trust that God will go before us when we step out in obedience. "Stepping out" in the church needs to be done with wisdom and good sense. One minister, without warning, impulsively announced during a Sunday worship service that anyone who wished to could remain after the service to receive healing prayers and anointing. Most of the congregation stayed! Going about it that way is possibly imprudent, but the story does suggest that we shouldn't timidly underestimate people's readiness to venture forth in healing. Nor should we underestimate the Spirit's influence in preparing the way.

A Closer Look at Three Structures for Healing Ministry

The following brief descriptions, plus the accompanying recommendations for further study, should help you think concretely about one or more specific forms a healing ministry might take in your own church.

Public worship. In the context of the regular service of worship, a *general prayer for healing* can be offered. This can be included in the prayers of intercession. Or a prayer can *name specific needs* that have been solicited beforehand, a practice requiring tact but building trust and support within the congregation.

Prayers for healing can become a prominent part of the service. A common pattern is for the worship leader to *invite worshipers to come to the altar* or communion rail near the end of the service in order to have the minister(s) lay hands on them and offer a prayer for healing. Either the same prayer can be said for each person or an extemporaneous prayer tailored to the request of each individual who comes forward. Anointing with oil may accompany the praying and laying on of hands. Another pattern for a worship service is that of trained healing teams of two or three people stationed at the altar or about the sanctuary to receive those who come for prayers.

A number of denominations include *orders for public services of healing* in their books of worship.[5] These services have the advantage of making healing the central theme of the whole service and are usually used either on a regular but infrequent basis, or on special occasions. Some churches have public services of healing one Sunday evening a month.

One of the most central means of healing in the church is the *sacrament of Holy Communion.* The service can readily be adapted to include prayers for healing and even laying on of hands and anointing. Even without these special prayers, many find the Eucharist a time when they experience the healing presence of Christ in a special way. One pastor holds an eight o'clock Eucharistic service with healing prayers every Sunday morning before the regular eleven o'clock service. He says the early service consistently nourishes him.

Building acts of healing into a church's public worship communicates that healing has been placed at the center of the church's ministry. Through its central acts of worship the church shows itself to be a healing community.

Healing prayer groups. Most churches have prayer groups of various sorts, but the groups considered in this book specifically and intentionally focus on praying for healing. These groups meet regularly—perhaps once every week or two—for at least an hour. The ideal size is six to eight people. They pray for those whose needs are made known to them, and they pray for each other. They can pray for the healing of institutions as well as individuals. They can minister deeply to their own church by praying persistently and over time for its healing.

Healing teams. In addition to healing prayer groups that pray *for* people, there are healing teams. Teams here refers to people trained not only to pray *for* people but to pray *with* people as well. Picture a team as two to four people gathered about someone who has requested their prayers. They may pray with a person only once or, more likely, many times over a long period of time. Their own spiritual preparation, training, and motivation equips them to move with people into the depths of their woundedness. Team members need to be spiritually mature and emotionally healthy, with a clear sense of call to this ministry.

A team's training begins with praying for each other and experiencing God's healing. They learn to feel comfortable praying both aloud and in silence. They learn to listen to the people who will come for prayer and to the Spirit's direction on how to pray for each one. They listen, too, for the difference between the Spirit and their own inner "static."

It is wise for a prayer team not to focus upon how many people come to a prayer session, or on how many are healed, or even upon what the team wants for a given person. The focus should stay on what God wants to do.

There need to be ways of dealing with issues that come up for the team. They are wounded healers themselves and are in need of prayers, too. Praying for others will open up areas of pain in the team that must be dealt with.

Along the way, the healing team continues to discern and pray about what it is doing, and stays open to changing structures or style.

Because of the pain and stress that will be brought to healing teams, their burden becomes heavy at times. It is good for the team to find ways to lighten up and have fun together!

A Final Word: "I Send You Forth to Heal"

We began with Jesus' words to the man with a withered hand, "Stretch out your hand!" In those words we heard Jesus inviting us to stretch out our hands toward him and toward others. In the pages that followed we learned what is meant by healing; dealt with questions about the theory and practice of healing; looked at praying for the healing of ourselves, others, and the social order; and portrayed the church as the unique community where Christian healing happens. In all this we have been mentally and spiritually preparing ourselves to respond to Jesus' invitation.

As our exploration concludes, we turn to another scene from Jesus' ministry. This time we meet Jesus teaching, preaching, and healing in Galilee:

> And Jesus went about all the cities and villages, teaching in their synagogues and preaching the gospel of the kingdom, and healing every disease and every infirmity. When he saw the crowds, he had compassion for them, because they were harassed and helpless, like sheep without a shepherd. Then he said to his disciples, "The harvest is plentiful, but the laborers are few; pray therefore the Lord of the harvest to send out laborers into the harvest."[6]

We are struck by the way Jesus' most characteristic acts— teaching, preaching, and healing—are closely linked. We see Jesus' compassion for the crowds. We pick up his sense of urgency about the harvest. Perhaps we can see ourselves both as members of the helpless crowd and as potential laborers for the harvest. Then the scene changes:

> And he called to him his twelve disciples and gave them authority over unclean spirits, to cast them out, and to heal every disease and every infirmity. . . . These twelve Jesus sent out, charging them, ". . . preach as you go, saying, 'The kingdom of heaven is at hand.' Heal the sick, raise the dead, cleanse lepers, cast out demons. You received without pay, give without pay.' "[7]

Again, in the clearest terms, Jesus joins the act of healing to the task of preaching God's reign. He commissions the twelve to carry on his own ministry, giving them power to heal and authority over evil. In the boldest possible terms, he sends them forth to heal.

Picture the twelve listening incredulously to Jesus' commission, dumbfounded at the gift and challenge he is giving them. "Who are we to receive such a challenge?" they ask themselves. "Where will we get the strength?" Imagine the circle of the twelve parting, opening to include other disciples with other names—old and young, women and men—from every people under the sun. See the circle widen even more to include friends you admire, teachers, and role models of yours who have been channels of healing for you. See at last the circle widen to make a place for you among the disciples. Hear Jesus say directly to you, simply and firmly, "I send you forth to heal!"

As you imagine that scene, what other images, associations and thoughts arise? What emotions are stirred up? Welcome whatever comes to you, alert to next steps and new directions for your journey in healing.

Bob tells about leading a clergy workshop through this guided imagery exercise.

> Once I was leading a clergy workshop through this guided imagery exercise. Along with the other participants, I sat in silence hearing Jesus say to me, "Bob, I send you forth to heal." "What does that mean for me?" I thought. "I'm a teacher, not a pastor. I don't have a 'gift' of healing. Where is Jesus sending me?" I then became aware of the others in the room, ministers earnestly exploring what healing prayer meant for them. The realization came to me: "Jesus is calling me to be a healer by offering hospitality to healers!" I saw myself in my own place of vocation helping to prepare the ground and tend the growth of the church's healing ministry, which would be embodied in the ministers attending the workshop and other clergy and laity to follow. That insight continues to form part of my call.

Jesus speaks the words to each of us. Jesus sends forth every Christian to be a healer, by virtue of our baptism. What shape the call will take will vary according to our different gifts and the world's needs. Pause to listen as Jesus says in ways you will be able to hear, "I send you forth to heal."

Appendix

Praying for an Institution

This prayer sequence is useful when a group is engaged in a process of discernment and intercession for an institution. Please see chapter 5 for further discussion.

The following is read aloud.

Our faith is that

- [Name of Institution] is both called by God to [type of work or ministry] and is empowered by God to do its work.

- God knows what we need and is able to give us even "more than we can ask or think." Jesus taught us to come to God with our problems, as a child would come to a parent.

- God uses our particular energies, talents, and commitment. We are invited to engage fully in what God might be doing through us. As a rule, we are not simply to sit idly by while God works around us.

- Surrender to God's will is not so much "giving up" as "giving over" all things into God's hands.

- The faith to move mountains is not so much our trusting *that* a certain thing will happen as trusting *in God* to work lovingly and creatively in our problem.

- Christian intercessory prayer is not magic. Instead we seek God's will and God's way in a particular situation, and pray for that. It may mean giving up our agenda and being open to a surprising new direction.

- *Discernment is the process by which we seek God's will so that we may know what to pray for and what action we are to take.*

- In discernment we assume that the God who loves us passionately also yearns to communicate with us. Although we may encounter our own static, we trust that God is able to get through to us somehow in discernment.

Spend a few minutes sharing your reactions to these statements of faith. Then enter into prayer, using the format below. (The leader will read each item and pause often so that everyone has time to follow the directions.)

- Come to God with our needs and tell God as honestly as you can what you believe we need and how you feel about the need. Be honest here, admitting feelings of hopelessness, worry, confusion, anger, and the like. [SILENCE]

- Invite God to enter into our problem. Release the problem to God. Ask, "What should we pray for?" "What should we do?" [SILENCE]

- Try very hard to stop talking—even in your own head—and just sit in God's presence, with the expectation that God will work in some way. [SILENCE]

- Pay attention to what happens next within you: images, thoughts, memories, verses of scripture, physical sensations, plans of action, and the like. For now, trust that whatever emerges does so for a reason that is related to the issue at hand. Remember, we asked God to work in us! [SILENCE]

The leader may then direct the group as follows:

Write down in *just a few words* what occured to you. Then, share briefly what each of you sensed in your discernment. Is there an emerging direction for the group?

Let individual discernment and any group consensus shape and give direction to your prayers. Pray together.

Explore avenues for action through discussion, workshops, and the like.

Continue to pray for discernment and for the needs of the institution named. Trust that if your discernment is off the mark God will correct your impression if you remain open. Continue to give over the problem to God.

Notes

Chapter 1—Stretch Out Your Hand

1. Mark 3:1–5.
2. I don't know what happened to the man after he was discharged, so I can't say that the healing was permanent. I do know that several months after his discharge he had not been readmitted to the hospital. However, the impact of this dramatic answer to prayer—even if it was temporary—gave me the courage to pray again for healing.
3. In the experience of the authors, dramatic instantaneous healings are not the norm, but they do happen on occasion.
4. The most comprehensive history of Christian healing is Morton T. Kelsey, *Psychology, Medicine and Christian Healing: A Revised and Expanded Edition of Healing and Christianity* (San Francisco: Harper and Row, 1988), 83–201. We are indebted to that book in what follows.
5. *Against Celsus* I. 46, 67. Quoted in Kelsey, 120.
6. Kelsey, 158.
7. Ibid., 145ff.
8. Summa Theologica, III. 44.3. Quoted in Kelsey, 169.
9. *Institutes of the Christian Religion* IV. 18. Quoted in Kelsey, 17.
10. Quoted in Kelsey, 183.
11. Kelsey, 182–85.

Chapter 2—The Most Frequently Asked Questions About Healing

1. See, for example, Kenneth R. Pelletier, *Mind as Healer, Mind as Slayer* (New York: Delta, 1978); O. Carl Simonton, Stephanie

Matthews-Simonton, and James Creighton, *Getting Well Again* (New York: Bantam Books, 1980); Bernie S. Siegel, *Love, Medicine and Miracles* (New York: Harper and Row, 1986).

2. See, for example, Fritjof Capra, *The Tao of Physics* (Berkeley: Shambhala, 1975); Gary Zukav, *The Dancing Wu Li Masters: An Overview of the New Physics* (New York: Bantam Books, 1979).

3. For a Process Theology interpretation of miraculous healing, see Barry L. Winston, *Evil and the Process God* (New York and Toronto: Edwin Mellen Press, 1985), 124–31.

4. See also Job 5:18. Death and illness are often represented as punishment for disobedience and sin: Deuteronomy 28:27–35; Genesis 20:1–17; Numbers 12; Psalms 32:3–4; 38:1–12; 41:4; 107:17–22.

5. See also 2 Kings 5:1–14.

6. Sometimes Jesus' Gethsemane prayer is a stumbling block for people who take it to mean they should not pray for healing. But see Francis MacNutt, *The Power to Heal* (Notre Dame, Ind.: Ave Maria Press, 1977), 134ff.

7. More recently the lines have blurred among fundamentalist, evangelical, and charismatic Christians regarding healing. See James Barr, *Fundamentalism* (Philadelphia: Westminster Press, 1977), 207–9.

8. See "Healing: The Church's Story" in chapter 1.

9. See Robert McAfee Brown, *Spirituality and Liberation: Overcoming the Great Fallacy* (Philadelphia: Westminster Press, 1988).

10. We address this issue in chapter 5.

11. See the helpful discussion of this in MacNutt, *Healing* (Altamonte Springs, Fla.: Strang Communications Co., 1988), 119–25.

12. See also Matthew 7:7–11; 18:19–20.

13. Space does not permit a full treatment of these texts. On the healing stories of the Gospels see R. H. Fuller, *Interpreting the Miracles* (London: SCM Press, 1963); Herman Hendrickx, *The Miracle Stories of the Synoptic Gospels* (London: Geoffrey Chapman, 1987).

14. On Jesus' "forceful and imaginative speech," see Robert C. Tannehill, *The Sword of His Mouth* (Philadelphia: Fortress Press, 1975).

15. See the figure of Job, for example, prior to Job 41:7; also Jeremiah (Jeremiah 15:15–21), and Paul (2 Corinthians 12:7–10).

16. Behind this question lies the deeper issue of suffering and divine will. In chapter 3 we consider the relation of suffering and healing.

17. The phrase "an environment conducive to healing" is adapted from Bernie Siegel, *Love, Medicine and Miracles* (New York: Harper and Row, 1986), 112.

18. We discuss spiritual discernment in chapter 3.

19. For discussions of why healing does not happen, see MacNutt,

Healing, 255–68; and James K. Wagner, *Blessed to Be a Blessing* (Nashville: The Upper Room, 1980), 64–76.

20. See endnote 4 above.
21. This is the subject of chapter 6.

Chapter 3—Praying for the Person God Is Calling Me to Be

1. For further discussion see references given in chapter 2, endnote 19.
2. Excellent resources for exploring the problem of suffering are Richard Vieth, *Holy Power, Human Pain* (Bloomington, Ind.: Meyer-Stone Books, 1988) and Vieth, *God, Where Are You? Suffering and Faith* (New York: United Church Press, 1989).
3. Vieth, *Holy Power, Human Pain*, 33.
4. Ibid., 31.
5. Matthew Linn, Sheila Fabricant, and Dennis Linn, *Healing the Eight Stages of Life* (New York: Paulist Press, 1988).
6. Ignatius of Loyola, *The Spiritual Exercises of Ignatius Loyola: A Literal Translation and a Contemporary Reading* (St. Louis: Institute of Jesuit Resources, 1978).
7. Scripture, tradition, experience, and reason are specifically named as the four formative factors of theology in *The Book of Discipline of the United Methodist Church* (Nashville, 1988), 81–86.

    See also John Maquarrie, *Principles of Christian Theology* (New York: Scribners, 1977), 4–18.
8. See Abraham Schmitt, *Before I Wake . . ., Listening to God in Your Dreams* (Nashville: Abingdon Press, 1984).
9. See Jerome Neufelder and Mary C. Coelho, eds., *Writings on Spiritual Direction by Great Christian Masters* (Minneapolis: Seabury Press, 1982), 117–39.
10. Fritz Perls, the founder of Gestalt therapy, often told his students "the hardest thing in the world to give up is your suffering."
11. Bernie S. Siegal, M.D., *Love, Medicine, and Miracles* (New York: Harper and Row, 1986), 65–99.

    See also O. Carl Simonton, M.D., Stephanie Matthews-Simonton and James L. Crighton, *Getting Well Again* (New York, Bantam, 1980), 107–13.
12. Francis MacNutt, *The Power to Heal* (New York: Bantam, 1977), 10–28.
13. There are many good resources for the exploration of faith imagination, sometimes called "healing of memories" or "inner healing." Three good ones are Matthew Linn, Dennis Linn, and Sheila Fabricant, *Prayer Course for Healing Life's Hurts* (New York: Paulist Press, 1983); Francis MacNutt, *Healing* (Altamonte Springs, Fla.:

Strang Communications Co., 1988), 181–97; Theodore Elliott Dobson, *Inner Healing, God's Great Assurance* (New York: Paulist Press, 1978).

14. See for example Matthew 12:22–45; 17:14–21; and Luke 4:33–37.
15. Luke 9:1.
16. See for example Romans 8:35–39 and Colossians 1:11–20.
17. Francis MacNutt, *Healing* (New York: Bantam, 1974), 215–37; Matthew and Dennis Linn, *Deliverance Prayer* (New York: Paulist Press, 1981); Don Basham, *Deliver Us from Evil* (Lincoln: Va.: Chosen Books, 1972); Kenneth McAll, *Healing the Family Tree* (London: Sheldon Press, 1982).

Chapter 4—A Simple Gift: Praying for Another's Healing

1. Dennis Linn, Matthew Linn, and Sheila Fabricant, *Praying with Another for Healing* (New York: Paulist Press, 1984), 3–5.
2. Henri Nouwen, *The Wounded Healer* (Garden City, N.Y.: Image Books, 1979).
3. We will further discuss healing teams in chapter 6.
4. It is ideal to be able to spend enough time with people individually to hear them out before praying with them. Sometimes this is not possible, such as during a healing service in which many people await prayer. At such times we must depend even more fully on the Holy Spirit to supply what we lack.
5. Thomas Gordon, *P.E.T.: Parent Effectiveness Training* (New York: Plume, 1970). For a discussion of this kind of listening, see chapter 3, "How to Listen So Kids Will Talk to You: The Language of Acceptance." Although this chapter is about listening to children, the principles are the same when listening to adults.

Chapter 5—Praying for the Social Order

1. Quoted in Kenneth L. Bakken, *The Call to Wholeness: Health as a Spiritual Journey* (New York: Crossroad, 1985), 8.
2. "The idea of peace as individual spiritual peace with God or internal peace of mind is not an Old Testament idea." "Peace," *Harper's Bible Dictionary* (New York: Harper and Row, 1985), 766.
3. Martin Noth, *Exodus* (Philadelphia: Westminster Press, 1962), 129.
4. See Walter Brueggemann, "Theological Education: Healing the Blind Beggar," *Christian Century* (February 1986): 114–16.
5. Walter Wink calls Jesus' temple cleansing "the paradigmatic collective exorcism in the New Testament"; *Unmasking the Powers: The Invisible Forces That Determine Human Existence* (Philadelphia: Fortress Press, 1986), 65.

6. George McClain, "Social Exorcism," *Journey Toward Justice: Commemorating the 80th Anniversary of the Social Creed of the People Called Methodists* (Staten Island, N.Y.: The Methodist Federation for Social Action, 1988), 116–33. The mailing address is MFSA, 76 Clinton Ave., Staten Island, NY 10301.
7. Ibid., 117.
8. Ibid., 116.
9. Ibid., 119.
10. Ibid., 123.
11. Ibid., 125.
12. Ibid., 127.
13. Ibid., 129.
14. Ibid., 132. The reference is to Walter Bruggemann, *Hopeful Imagination: Prophetic Voices in Exile* (Philadelphia: Fortress Press, 1986), 17ff.
15. Christians of South Africa have long recognized the spiritual dimensions of the struggle against apartheid. See, for example, the sermon of Allan Boesak, "I Have Seen Satan Fall," *If This Is Treason, I Am Guilty* (Grand Rapids: Eerdmans, 1987), 125–34.
16. Wink, *Unmasking the Powers*, 64ff.

Chapter 6—The Church as a Healing Community

1. James 5:13–16 (authors' inclusive language translation).
2. Philippians 4:15–18, passim (italics added).
3. For lay study of the Gospel healing stories, see Herman Hendrickx, *The Miracle Stories of the Synoptic Gospels* (London: Geoffrey Chapman, 1987).
4. Good books for lay study of healing are James K. Wagner, *Blessed to Be a Blessing* (Nashville: The Upper Room, 1980); Francis MacNutt, *Healing* (Altamonte Springs, Fla.: Strang Communications Co., 1988); Francis MacNutt, *The Power to Heal* (Notre Dame, Ind.: Ave Maria Press, 1977).
5. For example, *Book of Worship: United Church of Christ* (New York: United Church of Christ Office for Church Life and Leadership, 1986); *Occasional Services: A Companion to the Lutheran Book of Worship* (Minneapolis: Augsburg; and Philadelphia: Board of Publication of the Lutheran Church in America, 1982); *The Book of Common Prayer* (Episcopal) (New York: Seabury Press, 1979).
6. Matthew 9:35–38.
7. Matthew 10:1–8, passim.

Bibliography

Bakken, Kenneth L. *The Call to Wholeness: Health as a Spiritual Journey.*
New York: Crossroad, 1985. A Christian healer and physician stresses
the interrelationship of body, mind, and spirit.

Dobson, Theodore. *Inner Healing: God's Great Assurance.* New York:
Paulist Press, 1978. Emphasizes faith imagination and the healer's
discernment.

Edwards, Tilden. *Spiritual Friend: Reclaiming the Gift of Spiritual Direction.*
New York: Paulist Press, 1980.

Fuller, Reginald H. *Interpreting the Miracles.* London: SCM Press, 1963.

Hendrickx, Herman. *The Miracle Stories of the Synoptic Gospels.* New
York: Harper and Row, 1986. Both Fuller and Hendrickx use good New
Testament scholarship to study the Gospel healing stories.

Kelsey, Morton T. *Psychology, Medicine and Christian Healing: A Revised
and Expanded Edition of Healing and Christianity.* San Francisco: Harper
and Row, 1988. Traces the history of Christian healing from its biblical
roots to today's holistic perspective.

Linn, Dennis, and Matthew Linn. *Healing Life's Hurts: Healing Memories
Through the Five Stages of Forgiveness.* New York: Paulist Press, 1978.
Systematically based on Kübler-Ross's five stages of dying.

———. *Healing of Memories: Prayers and Confession-Steps to Inner Healing.*
New York: Paulist Press, 1974. A how-to book for personal or group
study.

Linn, Dennis, Matthew Linn, and Sheila Fabricant. *Praying with Another
for Healing.* New York: Paulist Press, 1984. A good introductory
workbook.

MacNutt, Francis. *Healing.* Rev. ed. Altamonte Springs, Fla.: Strang
Communications Co., 1988. Still the basic book on healing today, rich

in practical and theological insight. The revised edition is addressed to an ecumenical audience.

———. *The Power to Heal*. Notre Dame, Ind.: Ave Maria Press, 1977. A fresh and valuable supplement to *Healing*.

Pattison, Stephen. *Alive and Kicking: Towards a Practical Theology of Illness and Healing*. London: SCM Press, 1989. A British theologian argues for a Christian theology of healing that is socially and politicaly engaged and consistent with a modern worldview.

Schmitt, Abraham. *Before I Wake: Listening to God in Your Dreams*. Nashville: Abingdon Press, 1984. A good beginning book on personal dream work by a psychologist.

Siegel, Bernie S. *Love, Medicine and Miracles*. New York: Harper and Row, 1986. This physician's work with "exceptional patients" offers evidence for the power of the mind to heal the body.

Wink, Walter. *Naming the Powers: The Language of Power in the New Testament*. Minneapolis: Augsburg/Fortress, 1984.

———. *Unmasking the Powers: The Invisible Forces that Determine Human Existence*. Minneapolis: Augsburg/Fortress, 1986. Wink is a New Testament scholar who offers a perspective on the reality of spiritual and social evil.

Wise, Robert L. *When There Is No Miracle: Finding Hope in Suffering and Pain*. Ventura, Calif.: Regal Books, 1978. An honest and faithful look at this important pastoral subject in the healing ministry.

Journals

The Journal of Christian Healing. Published by The Institute for Christian Counseling and Psychotherapy, 103 Dudley Ave., Narberth, Pa. 19072. An excellent interdenominational and interdisciplinary journal for professionals desiring to integrate healing prayer with their work.

Weavings: A Journal of the Christian Spiritual Life. Published by The Upper Room, 1908 Grand Ave., P.O. Box 189, Nashville, Tenn. 37202.

Stretch Out Your Hand

Exploring Healing Prayer

Leader's Guide

Tilda Norberg
and
Robert D. Webber

A Kaleidoscope Series Resource

United Church Press
Cleveland, Ohio

Thank you for agreeing to lead a group in exploring healing prayer. In the spirit of Jesus' words to the man with the withered hand—"Stretch out your hand!"—you will be helping people stretch their minds and hearts, as well as their hands. You may feel this is quite a "stretch" for you too! *Stretch Out Your Hand* can be used with an ongoing group meeting weekly over a period of six weeks. The sessions that follow are designed to be used in six two-hour group meetings. The book also lends itself to use on a weekend retreat, where there is time between group sessions for personal reading and reflection. Feel free to revise the design of the sessions in the interest of your group's emerging agenda.

Before the Course Begins: Preparation for the Leader

Well in advance of the course, be sure every participant has a copy of the book and reads the first chapter before the first session.

Then, you will need to find a comfortable place to meet, the more homelike and private, the better. For each session, you will need a chalk-board or newsprint and a VCR and video monitor. Either provide paper for journal writing or ask people to bring their own. For some sessions it will helpful if participants have Bibles to refer to.

As leader you should read the participant's book as well and view the videotape ahead of time, so that you have an overview of the course.

Prayerful Preparation. This course is meant to be a journey of the spirit as well as an exploration of ideas. Therefore, it is crucial to prepare by praying in simplicity that the Holy Spirit will be present in the sessions. Pray daily for the course and for each participant individually. You might request that others join you in this and perhaps ask that the course be mentioned during intercession time in services of worship.

As you pray, know that you are not responsible for making anything significant happen for people, nor do you have to supply answers to questions. Depend on the Holy Spirit to be the true teacher of the course. *A relaxed and permissive style of group interaction is most conducive to exploring healing deeply.* To this end remember the following as the course proceeds:

- Your responsibilities as leader/servant of the group are to make necessary arrangements beforehand, to move the group process along within the given time frame, and to keep the discussion open and honest.
- You do not have to be an expert on healing. You don't have to be a theologian. Your role is simply that of helping your group explore healing for themselves.
- It will be helpful, but not necessary, for you to have experience in praying and in praying for healing. There are some suggested prayer exercises to lead in each session. The main thing is to be comfortable with the exercises, so that people catch your relaxed attitude. If you have not had personal experience with healing prayer, you may find reading one or more of the books in the bibliography helpful. Also, you may enlist coleaders who feel comfortable praying for healing.
- An attitude of openness on the leader's part is essential. Let it be all right with you if people have serious questions and doubts about things in the book. The goal of each session is not debate as an end in itself but prayerful listening; not changing people's minds but opening minds; not defending positions so much as allowing God to change us. Let loose ends of a discussion be.
- It is likely that some persons will bring questions that grow out of deep anguish. Questions like "Why didn't God heal my child? I prayed!" should never be met with quick, pat answers. It may happen that persons will cry as they share painful memories. Provide tissues, and let emotions be OK. Tears are often a gentle sign that God is at work.
- It is crucial that participants not feel coerced. Some may not be comfortable taking part in all the experiential workshop activities. Others may be put off by talking about certain ideas. Let it be all right with you for people to participate in their own ways. In fact, make it a point to say before each activity that persons

should feel free to "sit this one out" if they choose. Give up the idea that everyone has to do what the group is doing for the course to be successful.

- Encourage "I messages," that is, statements beginning with "I believe"; "I think"; "My experience is." Personal stories are wonderful "I messages." (Statements beginning "The truth is"; "Everyone knows"; "God says" are not "I messages"!) You can lead the way by being willing to share your own experiences.

- In any group there may be a few who tend to dominate or even derail the discussion. One way to deal with such persons is simply to thank them and then suggest that the group move on so that everyone gets a chance to speak.

- While trying to move the group along, be flexible. It may be more important to stay with a question or experience that is meaningful to the whole group at the moment than to stick slavishly to the agenda. Be as sensitive as you can to the feeling within the group and to the presence of the Spirit.

Chapter 1: Stretch out your Hand

Objectives of the Session. (1) To introduce the course and the writers of the resource book. (2) To encourage participants to reflect on their own prior experiences of and ideas about healing. (3) To stimulate thought on what Christian healing is, and is not. (4) To introduce the practice of faith imagination prayer.

As People Arrive. Provide newsprint and several colors of Magic Marker, or a chalkboard and chalk. As group members come in, make out name tags. On the chalkboard or newsprint, invite people to make "graffiti" (short) comments about the course, the reading they did, their hopes and fears, and to write down questions. Refer to these as people later introduce themselves.

Opening (10 minutes). Begin with a few familiar hymns, followed by a brief prayer for openness to God's work in the group. Then, invite people to be silent for a time as they center themselves in God's presence. End with the Lord's Prayer or perhaps another hymn.

Introductions (20–30 minutes).

1. Briefly introduce yourself as leader and speak personally about your hopes and expectations for the course. Explain the plan for the session.

2. View the first video segment.

3. Ask people to take *only a couple minutes* each to introduce themselves to the group and answer questions such as "What moved you to be here for this course—what curiosity or inner urging?" or "Briefly, what has been your experience of healing, however you define it?" or "What questions are on your mind right now?" Encourage as much openness as people can muster. As each one finishes, thank her or him. (If the group is large, this may be done better in groups of five or six, in the interest of time).

Faith Imagination: Guided Imagery Prayer (15 minutes). Begin by asking people to get comfortable and to close their eyes. State that they will be imaginatively entering into a scene from the Bible. Encourage them not to censor or edit what comes to mind but to allow images, sensations, sounds, and feelings to surface. The purpose of this exercise is to present a way to listen to the Holy Spirit. (For more information about this way of praying, see Anthony de Mello, S.J., *Sadhana: A Way to God* [St. Louis: The Institute of Jesuit Sources, 1978]. Other resources on faith imagination are listed in chapter 3, endnote 13. Whether or not you have participated in guided imagery exercises before, you may want to practice with a friend before the session.)

As leader, be aware that your timing is important. Read aloud slowly with pauses, allowing time for silence. However, if you speak too slowly, minds may wander. Do the exercise yourself even as you lead it, so that the pacing will occur naturally.

Invite people to close their eyes, to relax, and to pay attention to their breathing. Then, read slowly the first five paragraphs of chapter 1—the story of the man with a withered hand. Continue by saying: "Now, imagine *yourself* in that scene, only now *you* become the one to whom Jesus says, 'Stretch out your hand.'

[Pause.] What is your response? [Pause.] Do you feel afraid? [Pause.] hopeful? [Pause.] What in you is Jesus asking you to hold out to him for healing? What memory, emotion, relationship, bodily illness?" [Pause.] After a minute or two of silence, conclude: "You may not be finished hearing what Jesus has to say to you. But knowing that you can return to this scene at any time, return now to this place as you are ready."

Sharing Reactions (10–15 minutes). In pairs, speak to the following questions: "What did you discover in this prayer experience?" "What moved you?" "What do you think God was saying to you?" "Is this imagining, prayer?" Then, bring the group together to share significant insights with each other.

Neck and Shoulder Rub (20 minutes).

1. Ask people to find a partner, someone with whom they feel comfortable.

2. Ask person A to give person B the very best two-minute neck and shoulder rub he or she is capable of. They do this in silence.

3. At the end of two minutes have them pause, with hands still on their partner's neck or shoulders. Invite the A's to pray that their hands will be used by the Holy Spirit for the healing of their partner. All the B's invite the Holy Spirit to come to them through their partner's hands.

4. When you sense that people have indeed prayed their silent prayers, ask them to resume the neck and shoulder rubs for another two minutes.

5. Then switch roles without discussion and go through the procedure again, with person B giving a neck and shoulder rub to person A, first without prayer, then with prayer—two minutes each.

6. At the conclusion, ask the partners to talk to each other about what they discovered in doing this exercise. What differences did they note between the massage with prayer and without? What differences did they notice between giving and receiving? After a few minutes, let these discoveries be shared in the whole group.

What Healing Is and Is Not (30–40 minutes). The experiential exercises are a natural lead-in to a discussion of the definition of healing given on page 15, as well as to the story of Mary and to the video segment. Let the discussion focus particularly on the definition of healing. Begin by asking people to turn to page 15.

Slowly read aloud the statement of "what Christian healing is." Then ask people to think about the statement in light of three questions: (1) "What stands out to you in this statement?" (2) "What feels true?" (3) "What important ideas are missing for you?" Discuss the healing statement, either in three's or in the whole group, by responding to these questions. Encourage lots of participation. As people speak, list on the chalkboard or newsprint the key phrases in their responses.

Looking Ahead to the Next Session. Explain that the next session focuses on important questions about healing. Ask people to do the following at home in addition to reading chapter 2. (1) "Select the two or three questions within the chapter that are closest to your own most serious questions. Rewrite them in your own words, if necessary, in order to make them your own." (2) "List your own serious questions that are *not* included in the chapter." (3) "Live with these questions during the time before the next session. In journal writing and in prayer and meditation, look at these questions from various perspectives, seek insight into them, talk about them to friends."

Closing. Join hands in a circle and close with a simple prayer of thanks and sending forth.

Chapter 2: The Most Frequently Asked Questions About Healing

Objectives of the Session. (1) To air each person's genuine questions about healing. (2) To give permission to have and to raise significant questions. (3) To help each other deal with questions. (4) To experience Jesus' healing through faith imagination.

Overview of the Session. The focus of this session is upon creating an open environment for airing people's questions. This should not be simply a "head trip," however. Encourage the discussion to be personally relevant. Also, the experiential exercises at the end will provide a balance between talking about and directly experiencing healing prayer.

Opening (10 minutes). After singing a hymn, open with a time of silence for inner quieting followed by a brief prayer.

Follow-up (10–15 minutes). Allow time for anyone to share any thoughts or feelings about the last session or to tell what's happened to them in the intervening time. Do this with a minimal amount of discussion.

Identifying Our Questions (30–45 minutes). Refer to pages 17–18, where the seventeen questions are listed. Take a short time to clarify questions not clear, without answering them.

Form groups of three, and give each person five to ten minutes to speak in detail about one or two questions that are especially "theirs." Let them explain at length the experiences they have had that relate to their question. The other members of their small groups are to listen and help the person only to express him- or herself fully. After five to ten minutes, change the roles until everyone has had a chance to speak.

Call the groups together and allow the people to repeat significant ideas. Note these on the board, and note which ones most people have in common. According to the time available, allow dialogue among those in the group to flow as it will.

Encounter with a Sick Boy's Father (Mark 9:14–29) (30–40 minutes). (1) Ask people to look in their Bibles at Mark 9:14–29. Slowly read the passage aloud. (2) View the second video segment. (3) Gather in groups of three to five to discuss the following questions (write the questions for all to see): (a) "What kinds of faith and lack of faith do you see in the story?" (b) "Is the father a person of faith? Explain." (c) "Do you identify with the father? Do your questions about healing show an affinity to the father's faith or lack of faith?"

Optional Prayer Exercise (10 minutes). Invite your group to participate in this simple experiment in praying for another person. The goal is to see how simple and undramatic it is to pray for another (though persons prayed for frequently notice a change in their condition rather quickly!). Ask if there is someone with a minor physical ailment (headache, cold) who would like to receive the prayers of the group. If there is, ask that person to be seated where others who wish to participate may gather about, lay their hands gently upon her or him, and pray with either simple words or no words at all, as they are led. When the prayers seem at an end, ask the people to return to their seats.

Let everyone, including the one prayed for, talk about the experience.

Closing. Close with one verse of a familiar hymn, sentence prayers, or the Lord's Prayer.

Chapter 3: Praying for the Person God Is Calling Me to Be

Objectives of the Session. (1) To relate healing prayer to the mystery of human suffering, to the process of spiritual discernment, and to the unity of body, mind, and spirit. (2) To help people discern more fully the person God is calling him or her to be, and to pray for that emerging self.

Overview of the Session. Chapter 3 contains ideas central to understanding and practicing healing prayer for oneself. The session is intended to provide ample opportunity for free-flowing discussion, in which persons relate the ideas and stories of the chapter to their own experience. The guided imagery exercise(s) and the video segment support this free exchange of thoughts and feelings.

Opening (10 minutes). Gather in silence for a time; then slowly read Mark 5:24b–34, the story of the woman who touched Jesus' garment. Invite the group to continue in silence while reflecting on this woman as a model of those who boldly ask Jesus for what they need.

Introducing the Topic (30 minutes). View the third video segment. On the board list, together with the group, the important ideas in praying for one's own healing. Be sure to include (1) the key ideas arising from the definition of healing, (2) the issue of suffering and healing, and (3) the idea of discernment. Suffering, especially, can become a central issue as we pray for healing. It needs to be treated with both humility and confidence in God's care for each person. Let the group discuss suffering fully, trusting their wisdom to find a faithful, if incomplete, resolution.

I Need to Touch His Garment Because . . . (60 minutes). Referring back to the story of the woman, invite people to enter into a leisurely process of personal discernment and prayer, in which they discern what in them needs healing at this time. Describe the process through which you will be leading the group. Then ask them to form into small groups of three. They should choose two other persons with whom they will feel comfortable sharing something of themselves. Emphasize that they should not feel pressured to relate anything that will make them uncomfortable.

1. Working alone with pencil and paper for two minutes, each person completes the sentence, "I need to touch Jesus' garment because . . ." Remind people to include in their thinking any kind of healing—of body, emotions, memories, attitudes, relationships.

2. In groups of three, each person takes five to ten minutes to speak about what came to him or her in the previous two minutes. As one person speaks, the other two listen, with one ear to the person and the other ear to the Spirit, and respond as they feel led. For example, they should try to help the speaker discover if a physical need has emotional and spiritual dimensions, or vice versa. After ten minutes the roles change, until all three have had a chance to speak.

3. Without a break or further comment, in silence for five minutes, use the individual discernment process outlined in chapter 3. Facilitate this by reading aloud the ten steps of discernment (beginning on page 39) as the others in silence follow your directions. Leave enough time between steps for each person to respond.

4. After individual discernment, ask the groups to form again in order to report briefly what they discerned about their own need for healing. If they are comfortable doing so, each person tells his or her companions what to pray for. Then, the other two place their hands on the person and pray, silently or quietly aloud, simple prayers for healing.

5. When the small groups have finished, invite them together again to report whatever aspects of this exercise they are comfortable sharing with the whole group.

Bringing Things Together (20 minutes). Ask people to shift gears a bit now. State something like the following: "In light of the experience of discernment and healing prayer we have just completed, look again at the key phrases in the definition of healing in chapter 1. Also, look again at your own questions about healing from the previous session. For example, do you sense personally that God is actively involved in your growth; that the Spirit is continually at work in you, not zapping you from outside; that God yearns to bring you to wholeness? Can you identify with Lois, who prays that God will 'grow' her? Or with Kathleen, who is still in need of healing, still on her journey, but joyful in her discovery of renewed faith?" Through such questions, encourage a dialogue to synthesize thoughts and experiences.

Closing. Form a circle and hold hands. Invite sentence prayers, ending with the Lord's Prayer.

Chapter 4: A Simple Gift: Praying for Another's Healing

Objectives of the Session. (1) To think of many settings in which participants can pray for another's healing. (2) To explore the preparation and the practical steps for praying for another's healing. (3) To explore the healing potential of anointing with oil.

Materials for the Session. In addition to a chalkboard, VCR, and monitor, provide a few teaspoons of olive oil in a cruet, plus vessels (saucers or small cups are fine) to put it in, one vessel for every five to eight people in the class.

Opening (5 minutes). Open with singing and a brief prayer. Ask people to mention any persons who need prayers for healing. Ask the group to keep these people in mind for a later time in the session.

Bringing Another to Jesus (20 minutes). Invite the group to enter into a guided imagery exercise in which they bring a friend or loved one to Jesus.

When people are seated with their eyes closed, give the following directions:

1. "In silence, prayerfully ask the Spirit to show you who needs your prayers most at this moment—a friend or family member, someone you know personally. They may need healing of spirit, emotions, or body; you may not even know what their brokenness is. Wait to see who comes most persistently to mind." [Pause.]

2. "Imagine you are with your friend in an open field on a beautiful day. [Pause.] A short distance away, Jesus is speaking to a

small group of people. You bring your friend to the group, which opens to make room for you both. [Pause.] Soon, Jesus turns his full attention to you, and you tell him all about your friend, and his or her needs. Jesus listens compassionately. [Pause.] Then, Jesus turns his attention to your friend. [Pause.] Now, for a few minutes, watch to see how Jesus responds. [Allow two or three minutes of silence.] As you prepare to leave your friend there with Jesus, ask Jesus what *you* are to be doing to help your friend. Hear what Jesus says to you. Then leave them there together. [Pause.] As you are ready, open your eyes."

3. In groups of two or three, invite people to share their experiences, especially any surprises in Jesus' dealings with their friends or any discoveries of ways they are to participate in their friends' healing. As there is time, allow for some general sharing with the whole group.

Many Ways of Praying for Another's Healing (30 minutes). View the fourth video segment.

Together or in small groups, ask participants to express their reactions to the video's presentation of ways of praying for others' healing.

As appropriate, direct the discussion to broader questions: "At this point in the course, where are you in your understanding of healing? Think back to the definition of healing in chapter 1. Is your thinking changing about any of the things said there? Recall the questions of chapter 2. What's happening with your questions? How are you relating your *understanding* of healing to your *experience* of healing prayer?" This last question is particularly important.

Discerning How to Pray for Another (30–45 minutes). The purpose of this exercise is to give people a taste of praying with discernment for another. Praying with discernment is both simple and potentially powerful. In preparation, refer to the ten steps of discernment beginning on page 39. Then, in small groups of three or four, have one member of the group volunteer to be the focus of the group's discernment and prayer. The volunteers take a few minutes to tell about what in their life they feel needs prayers—some place of physical, emotional, or spiritual broken-ness. Following the steps of discernment, the other members of the group listen for guidance as to how to pray. They share their insights, check them with the focal person, then pray for him or her, laying on hands as they feel led. Afterward, they talk about anything that has happened to them.

As time allows, repeat the process with another volunteer from the small groups.

Practicing Anointing (20 minutes). A natural follow-up to the previous exercise is to offer anointing with oil to those who wish to receive it. In preparation, emphasize that this is not a magical rite and that one does not have to be ordained to anoint another in the name of Jesus Christ.

1. Holding the cruet or vessel(s) of oil, pray a simple prayer of blessing, such as: "Bless this oil, O Lord, that it may become for us a means of your healing love"; or "O God, send your Spirit upon us and upon this oil, that those who receive it may be made whole according to your will."

2. Form groups of five to eight persons, with each group seated in a circle around an empty chair. Place oil beside each empty chair.

3. As persons are ready, they take the empty chair and say for what they desire healing prayers—for themselves or for another person. Another member of the group who feels led to do so dips a thumb or fingertip in the oil, makes the sign of the cross upon the person's forehead or hand, and says simply, "[Name], I anoint you for healing, in the name of Jesus Christ." Others then may want to gather around the person, lay their hands on her or him, and pray briefly, silently or aloud. When that person has taken his or her seat, another person may occupy the center chair, and so on, until all who wish to be anointed have been.

After the anointing, give people who wish to talk about the experience time to do so.

Closing. Form the group in a circle. Close with a brief prayer.

Chapter 5: Praying for the Social Order

Objectives of the Session. (1) To explore the distinctive spiritual resources of Christian faith for healing the brokenness of social institutions. (2) To practice a group exercise of social healing.

Opening (5 minutes). Sing one or two familiar hymns, followed by a time of silence. Read aloud, slowly, John 2:13–17 (Jesus driving the money changers from the temple).

Introducing the Idea of Social Healing (30–40 minutes). If you wish to introduce the subject on a personal note, give some of your own reactions to the ideas of chapter 5. Mention both what you find significant and what confuses you or what turns you off about social healing.

View the fifth video segment.

Invite the group to discuss, first in groups of five, then all together, the following questions: (1) "If you know organizations that behaved like the 'drowned church,' do you think their problems were related to some past wound or institutional trauma?" "Do you think spiritual means such as those used by the prayer group might have helped them?" "What are the risks in trying something such as the prayer group tried?" (2) "If you can or cannot see yourself participating in George McClain's social exorcism, what are your main thoughts and feelings about it?" (3) "A premise of the anti-apartheid exorcism was the 'agressive, God-denying' character of social evil. Does this understanding of evil make sense to you, and would you be prepared to act on it?" (4) "What do you think of the authors' central thesis, that social institutions and problems are appropriate objects of healing prayer?"

Group Exercise in Social Exorcism (45 minutes). Refer to "A Group Exercise in Social Exorcism" in the text (pages 80–81). In groups no larger than eight to twelve persons, go through the process outlined in those pages. Begin by having each group appoint a group facilitator. Within the group each person is to name, without discussion, one social influence that personally burdens or dehumanizes him or her. When all have had a chance to speak, each group is to agree upon one of the named social influences on which to focus for the remainder of the exercise. When a group has selected its focus, it is to follow—soberly, prayerfully, and expectantly—the five steps described in the text. Afterwards allow plenty of time for reflecting on the experience.

Follow-up Prayers for Others (5–15 minutes). Invite the group to identify persons for whom they would like the group to pray.

Instruct the group to be seated with eyes closed and then to imagine that the one(s) for whom they are praying are bathed in the light of God's healing love; or filled with the healing energy of the Holy Spirit; or surrounded as by a blanket of the Spirit's warm, healing presence. Maintain the image for some minutes, "soaking" the person.

Closing. Close with a hymn and a brief prayer.

Chapter 6: The Church as a Healing Community

Objectives of the Session. (1) To imagine the Christian church as a healing community. (2) To learn practical steps toward starting healing ministries in local churches. (3) To discover and deepen each participant's call to a ministry of healing.

Opening (5–10 minutes). Invite persons to suggest ways to open the session.

Praying for Others (0–15 minutes). If the group would like time to pray for specific persons, do so early in the session. Let the group members suggest a specific way to pray and perhaps take leadership in praying.

Envisioning the Church as a Healing Community (45–60 minutes). Through two brainstorming activities, help the group imagine possibilities for envisioning the church as a healing community.

1. Ask the group to imagine all possible ways a local congregation can be a healing community—to its own members, to persons and institutions in its community, and to the wider human community. List the ideas on the chalkboard or newsprint.

2. View the sixth video segment.

3. Form groups of three to five to discuss the following questions: "Dreaming a bit, what kinds of healing work would you like to see brought to birth in our church? Where do you fit into your dreams for the church?"

Strategizing Next Steps (20–40 minutes). Gather the whole group again. Ask people briefly to describe some of the concrete visions they have, especially ones that seem to have some urgency or timeliness. Note these ideas on the chalkboard or newsprint, grouping and categorizing them as best you can.

From this list, have the group identify a few common themes or ideas; then ask people to gather together in strategy groups around these common concerns. For example, the class may form groups to strategize the following: forming an adult study class on healing; including healing prayers in worship services; beginning a regular healing prayer group; recruiting and training healing teams; gathering resources on healing for the church library; learning more about specific issues; and so forth.

An Alternative Exercise. In place of the strategizing just described, a group might want to use the exercise "Praying for an Institution" (Appendix, page 97). This is readily adapatable for use as a tool for discerning what a congregation is to do in becoming a healing community.

As time is available, have groups report back.

Commissioning: I Send You Forth to Heal (20 minutes). Use pages 95–96 as the basis for a guided imagery exercise. Read Matthew 9:35–38 and 10:1, 5–8. Lead the group with their eyes closed through the visualization on those pages, adapting the words as you need to. Lead up to Jesus' saying to each one, "I send you forth to heal." At that point, invite persons to open themselves to what the Spirit is calling them to be and do as healers. Allow several minutes of silence. Finally, invite them to "return" to the room where you are. After a pause, give each person who wishes to speak about the experience a chance to do so.

Concluding Moments (10–20 minutes). If you want participants to fill out an evaluation of the course, this would be a good time for them to do it. At this time also it is important to give people a chance to speak about the entire experience of the class. Ask: "How have you grown? What's yet to be explored for you? What has happened to you?"

Close in a way that seems appropriate.

After the Course Is Over

It would be an appropriate follow-up to the course for the participants to come together for a service of worship that includes healing prayers. Course participants might want to invite others to attend with them. Consult the resources in the bibliography for model services and practical guidance.